Table of

C000195876

Introduction

I was raised in the 1970s and '80s—the apex of the processed, packaged, pre-made food era. My mother was (and still is) a lousy cook who, because of the combination of science, big business, and advertising, never learned how to cook properly. Dinner at our house, which I took over making for the family around age 10, consisted of opening a box or a can or a wrapper and heating up the contents. There were rare occasions when my mother 'cooked' but more often than not it wasn't a treasured heirloom recipe, but something clipped from a women's magazine or a free cookbook given away at the supermarket. These cookbooks were the source of millions of meals across the United States.

I can't say that we were fed by bad parents as much as by bad corporations. I remember a particularly awful main course devised by the Heinz Company featuring Heinz Ketchup: 'Glorified Hamburgers' consisted of ground beef seasoned with salt and pepper spread on a Wonder Bread bun, topped with a dollop of Heinz Ketchup, then baked (or broiled). They always came out burnt to a crisp at the edges and raw in the middle and were dubbed 'Gorified Hamburgers' by my father who had a talent for Spoonerisms.

One of my earliest memories is of my younger, then two-year-old sister throwing an epic temper tantrum in the backseat of a VW station wagon while driving the 250 miles to my grandmother's farm. The cause: a parental 'no' to her request for *another* serving of Pepsi in her baby bottle. My dad ended up pulling over to the side of the interstate to have my mother fill the bottle again after 20 miles of screaming. Many will scoff with disbelief at the anecdote, thinking that somehow it was impossible that in even in the dark ages of the 1970s, a parent would feed their baby soda pop.

a little *TRICK*

that makes a *TREAT*

SEVEN-UP IN MILK!

Mix chilled 7-Up and cold milk in equal parts, by pouring the 7-Up gently into the milk. Do not stir. The 7-Up adds a light and delicate flavor making a delicious blended food drink.

Mothers know that this is a wholesome combination. The addition of 7-Up gives milk a new flavor appeal that especially pleases children.

"FRESH UP" WITH SEVEN-UP!

Two advertisements from the "Nothing Does it Like 7-Up" campaign that suggested 7-Up was so 'pure and wholesome' that it was recommended for babies. / c. 1950s

The Great White Whale of mass consumerism from the 1950s to the financial collapse of the early 1980s was working and middle classes newly returned from World War II and their children. (Commonly referred to as the Greatest Generation and Baby Boomers, respectively.) Of course, on television, Mrs. Brady would have never allowed Alice to give the kids soda pop, but the Bradys were the aspirational upper-middle-class family no one in our neighborhood believed existed. If your dad worked a job that required physical labor, dollars to donuts you drank soda pop as a kid. It would have been impossible not to like Coke and Pepsi, and all the lesser brands that used the latest psychological techniques and ruthless business practices to ensure that kids and their parents bought the products.

We read newspaper stories of the obesity epidemic and dismiss it as a problem of individual intelligence, willpower, and culture. We talk about 'class' structures with a pearl-clutching concern that if people only *tried* a little harder, they could be richer, thinner, happier, and healthier. What's lost is the connection to our common and shared food history. Whether you're a Mayflower descendant or a recent immigrant, your American-ness is shaped by the actions of a small group of people and corporations who want you to behave in a way that serves them.

American advertising cookbooks, so ubiquitous in the 20th century, have given way to quick-speed Internet cooking videos and extreme recipes that wink at their awfulness and our predilection for 'bad' food. But for those 75 or so years we remember as the golden age of advertising, corporations drove the American diet to the deleterious effect we see today. How we got there is the story I want to tell.

Chiquita Banana Says /
1947 / United Fruit Company /
Ham Banana Rolls advertisement

Hamdinger advertisement / 1975 /
The Patrick Cudahy meat packing company
introduced this canned, pre-sliced ham
product as their answer to SPAM®. It wasn't
successful and production ended in 1979.

Cookbooks—
A Brief History

How did we get from hardtack to hamdingers? The story of American food is like the country itself, a tale of mix-ups, mash-ups, and too many disguised unsavory ingredients. What we think is the truth is often a fiction as invented as the foods we eat. Our immigrant ancestors lop a few letters off the end of some Eastern European orgy of consonants, and the Zalisczitzskies from beyond the pale become the Sharps of Upper East Side New York. We've become who we want to be—Americans—but we're a long way from Granny's cooking.

No one woke up one sunny morning in 1947 and decided to wrap a banana with a slice of ham, slather it with an eggy cheese sauce and serve it to their family. It's more than a recipe or a culinary fad (though these oddball recipes did become faddish). Cookbooks are the earliest documented writing and the earliest form of advertising. Before there was the 'word of God,' Babylonians wrote instructions on the proper way to make beer. Old recipes reflected what could be prepared safely with available fruits, vegetables, herbs, and meats, but as palates evolved and specialized skills developed and spread throughout the world, cooking became a skilled trade soon followed by the creation of cookbooks.

Tablet containing recipes / Babylon / c. 1750s B.C.

A recipe, in its most basic incarnation, is instructional, a listing of ingredients and procedures to allow for consistent reproduction of a particular food or combination of foods. Collect and organize them, and they become a cookbook. The earliest of cookbooks were random collections of either favored recipes or the explanation of a complicated technique. The Roman Apicius is cited as the first formal cookbook as it bears the familiar organization by type of ingredient. The Apicius is attributed to an unnamed first-century gourmand—the notes, recipes, and instructions reveal details of life at that time. Cookbooks then as often now were thought of as necessary but superfluous, not something a person of intellect or refinement would collect. There was, until the 20th century, a vast chasm between who cooked the food and who ate the food. The lower on the class scale one was, the more physical labor you did. Cooking was a job considered better than, say, privy maintenance, but still the responsibility of slaves and servants.

Early cookbooks were not intended for the servants to read (as most could not) but designed as a memory aid for stewards of the household. As eaters visiting neighboring estates, the lord or lady of the manor would charge stewards with acquiring recipes of favorite dishes from other families. Handwritten receipts were then compiled into hand-bound books, these cookbooks that were copied and passed along until the advent of the printing press.

Publishers saw cookbooks, again, valued as necessary but not highly regarded as an object, as a can't-miss moneymaker. The prolificacy of every local printer publishing a version of the town's most famous cookbook began the long tradition of plagiarism in cookbooks and the difficulty in determining true authorship of early recipes and cookbooks. Given a finite number of ingredients and methods of cooking, claiming a single person invented or wrote a recipe is problematic at best. Added to this mishmash is the fact that by the mid-1400s, women were most often the cooks and keepers of recipes, but not considered skilled nor intelligent enough to cook in the wealthiest of households. It isn't until the late 1500s that a woman was credited as an author of a cookbook (Anna Wecker, *Ein Köstlich new Kochbuch, tr. A Delicious New Cookbook*).

Ein Köstlichnew Kochbuch,
tr. A Delicious New Cookbook /
Anna Wecker / 1598 Edition

Calvinists, Pilgrims, and Cookbooks

e may think of America as a freedom-loving melting pot, and undoubtedly our palates reflect our insatiable hunger for new flavors, but the reality is that American culture is firmly rooted in her founding mythmakers—the Pilgrims. Cookbooks and household manuals as promulgated by these founders became a preferred tool for spreading not only their gospel but the strict rules for behavior becoming, in essence, the first advertising cookbooks. A review of Protestant separatism shows how cookbooks of collected recipes became a soft-power sales tool.

At the time of the colonists' arrival en masse in the mid-1600s, Europe—specifically England—was embroiled in wars fueled by dynasty and religion. The Protestant Reformation of the 1500s broke the centralized power of the Catholic Church, giving rise to local bishoprics and councils deciding how to interpret the Bible and dogmatic traditions. Throughout the hundred or so years between the reigns of Elizabeth I to the Restoration of Charles II, the English church roiled with proselytizers who succeeded in deposing the monarchy, starting a civil war, and generally bringing about the most far-reaching cultural ideas that still affect us today.

During the 1600s, the word Puritan was an insult used against those single-minded believers who felt their salvation in God was tied not just to personal purity, but that of the salvation of the world. To them, heaven was a place on Earth and must be brought about by force, if necessary, on unbelievers, heathens, and especially Catholics. Pilgrims had a slightly more nuanced belief—that they should indeed bring about God's kingdom on Earth, but to do it separately from existing society. All Pilgrims were Puritans, but not all Puritans were Pilgrims. There was no singular Protestant denomination under which they organized as traveling charismatic preachers walked the fertile soils of Albion spreading their 'good news.' To the poor and working classes, this new interpretation of the gospel was good news; it was a revolutionary idea that an individual could have a personal relationship with God and be assured a place in heaven. This idea was radically different from the Catholic dogma where salvation depended on the intercession of a holy priest of the Roman church.

Protestant churches vary slightly in their philosophical origins, each one having a differentiating practice or belief that sets them apart from the others. To the non-ecclesiastical laymen it may seem small and academic, but to believers these nuances are important. The influence of Calvinism (loosely defined by the notion of personal salvation, but also the idea that the 'saved' are selected by God and the only path to heaven was through their particular style of worship), informed many of the sects, including Methodism, Presbyterianism, Wesleyism, and Congregationalists. The Congregationalists were the English puritanical separatist group that became our American Pilgrims.

Women's roles in Protestant households grew in autonomy and responsibility as the Reformation took hold. Women were still subservient to God and man but enjoyed new power as they oversaw upholding the physical and moral health of the family according to Puritan dictums. A man may fall under the spell of demonic influence, but a woman was held to a higher standard of behavior as she was not only subject to the touch of evil but the absolute possession by the devil and his lesser minions. Puritan women were to be vigilant against any and all deviation from the will of God as dictated by her husband, the community elders, and pastor.

A critical element to the success of the entire community was that women could read. The Puritan vision of women's education was simple—that women were vessels for the Holy Spirit and all knowledge was used to achieve the goal of perfecting oneself as a reflection of God. Women were expected to educate their children to become perfect servants of the Lord. (Any additional education in Latin, mathematics, or the natural sciences was thought to be against the logical hierarchy of man and forbidden to women.)

As printing technology grew in its efficiencies, so too did the power wielded by the ascendant Reformationists; printed books were a potent method to share not only spiritual revelations, but the explicit instructions, sermons, and admonitions that were part and parcel of the Calvinist message. The second most popular type of book published by the nascent publishing industry, after Bibles, was the combined cookbook/household manual and this continued to grow in popularity as Protestantism spread throughout northern Europe.

The notion that dynastic family ties determine societal position is rooted in European aristocracy while the American myth that righteous, moral, and right behaviors are the sole determination of character and therefore one's place in society was a profound idea. It's the American version of Calvinism that God chooses only a few for special favor while everyone else can reap the benefits of lordly salvation by emulating Calvinist practices that informed our founders. Cookbooks became a sanctified method to educate all aspirants to a good and Christian life in the correct way to maintain a household. Over time these manuals and cookbooks lost some of their overt religiosity, but the moral tone and pre-scription for proper housekeeping and recipes remained.

There is much debate by food historians as to whether the Calvinist prohibitions extended to food. There may not be a definitive answer, as many Calvinist writers of the day contradicted each other depending on their particular interpretations of scripture. There is enough documentation to say that many Puritans believed that foods should be bland so as not to excite the senses and trigger lust as well as a few who took a purely oppositional stance to spiced foods from France and Italy, which smacked of Catholic excesses.

In analyzing recipes of the time and in comparison with modern Amish (a puri-tanical Anabaptist Calvinist Protestant sect originating in Switzerland and Ger-many) recipes, one sees a visible trend toward what is called 'Plain Cooking.' These recipes contain very few spices and are heavy in fat-laden sauces. These dishes may taste good, but can in no way be considered 'spicy.' Excised too were traditional references to 'folk wisdom' which were firmly in the realm of the devil. Gone were the customs of long-standing Christianized yet pagan traditions of sac-rifices to the earth for successful harvests. Medicinal recipes and fertility charms were also omitted by the Puritans but found their way back into the manuals in the 1800s. Newly added were quotes from Scripture to remind the woman of her sacred role in housekeeping. It was not a smooth transition as the Old Ways die hard.

The first century of the New England settlement saw clashes between rival colony groups and religious believers. New England history is pockmarked with instances of violence both unknown and infamous. We're familiar with the Salem witch trials, but there were other Puritan villages opposed to any lifestyle but their own. Non-Puritan settlers were allowed to live in these growing towns as servants but were expected to follow the restrictive laws and customs. As settlements grew into cities, English tolerance for the religious fervor of its North American colonies was tested when a group of Boston Puritans executed four Quakers in 1660. In the aftermath of the English Civil War, newly restored (and hedonistic, non-religious) King Charles II had little patience for fundamentalist repressions, and intervened in successive actions to defang the Puritan theocracy in America, eventually revoking their establishing Charter in 1684. It was the effective end of self-rule in America and the beginning of direct English colonization as royal governors and troops were sent to take over gov-erning the intransigent Puritans. Though out of governmental power, the century of Puritan rule left an indelible mark on American culture that reverberates throughout our food culture today.

Becoming Americans

As America grew in population, her citizens developed a sense of identity separate from the English colonizers. Earlier settlers from the Netherlands, Spain, and France intermingled with the New England settlers as all parties sought to expand their influence and land holdings. Ethnic and cultural strongholds grew into cities focused on a single unifying belief— trade and economic growth. The European migrants shared the view that Christianity was above any other religion and the right of dominion over the Earth was their birthright. This dogma included the unfortunately common belief that non-white people were of a different species and without souls and therefore 'lesser' and subject to the white settlers. The adverse effects of these Calvinist beliefs are felt today in the continual struggles to define the American identity.

The state of geopolitics in the mid-1700s was complicated. The 'Great Game' was on, as the intertwined European monarchies continued their race to colonize every inch of the planet. The American colonies shared the North American landmass with the territories controlled by France, Spain, and even Russia on the Pacific coast. Away from Europe, the new American ruling class was a distinct mix of Puritan Pilgrim descendants, Dutch traders, and casually Protestant plantation owners. Their collective economic concerns outweighed their differences—enough to unite against England and form their own country. All the factors were well-positioned for the American colony to break from English colonial rule.

Post-American revolution, household manual/cookbook creators sought to convey the increasingly unique American identity. The first entirely American cookbook was published in 1796 in Hartford, Connecticut, titled *American Cookery, or the art of dressing viands, fish, poultry, and vegetables, and the best modes of making pastes, puffs, pies, tarts, puddings, custards, and preserves, and all kinds of cakes, from the imperial plum to plain cake: Adapted to this country, and all grades of life.* Written by Amelia Simmons, *American Cookery* is an essential document in American history. Unlike the English cookbooks found in American kitchens at the time, this book was written by someone who was familiar with both English-influenced Puritan 'plain cooking' recipes, the Dutch-influenced 'cookey' baking of the Hudson Valley, as well as the fashionable French cuisine that used wines and spicing for flavor and included recipes from all cooking traditions using wholly American ingredients.

Ameila Simmons' American Cookery, or the art of dressing viands, fish, poultry, and vegetables, and the best modes of making pastes, puffs, pies, tarts, puddings, custards, and preserves, and all kinds of cakes, from the imperial plum to plain cake: Adapted to this country, and all grades of life. / 1796

The Virginia Housewife or
Methodical Cook /
Mary Randolph / 1838

Simmons' book was the first noted use of cornmeal instead of oats that transformed an English oatcake to the American Johnnycake.

Differing from the combined household manual/cookbooks of the era, she omits any housekeeping tips to focus solely on cooking. She explains, in her simple introduction, that this book is different from previous cookbooks and in doing so becomes the embodiment of the new American woman. She's an orphan; she's ambitious, she's conscientious of Calvinist modesty, but is willing to risk judgment for something delicious. Here she admonishes readers to not judge her, because she's an expert with experience and the recipes create delicious food: *"By having an opinion and determination, I would not be understood to mean an obstinate perseverance in trifles, which borders on obstinacy—by no means, but only an adherence to those rules and maxims which have stood the test of the ages, and will forever establish the female character, a virtuous character, although they conform to ruling taste of the age in cookery, dress, language, manners, etc."*

Simmons' book followed in the European tradition of cookbook plagiarism. Printers in America happily and unscrupulously published bootleg versions of Simmons' cookbook. Some would take the time to change a name or place to disguise the piracy, but more often than not, cookbooks existed in a nether realm of authorship. Even today, many recipes are vague in origin. As for Amelia Simmons, she collected recipes from her various jobs and co-workers, worked to refine them, and then wrote them all down. But in analyzing the actual recipes, we see a distinct through-line of cooking techniques and flavor combinations originating in the early Middle Ages.

Realizing that Simmons' name alone conveyed expertise and authenticity to book buyers, publishers sought to create more specifically American cookbooks with respected American voices. The American homemaker of the 1800s was still rooted in Calvinist-influenced Protestant culture but was also exposed to a wider range of cultural experiences. The recipes included in the next wave of American cookbooks began to reflect influences from the Southern states which had roots in West African and Native American cuisines. Enslaved peoples working on plantations cooked familiar foods with the ingredients on hand, often the scraps from the slave owner's house. These foods eventually traveled from the slave quarters to the master's house where they were absorbed into the English-inflected cuisine. Southern foodways have a complicated and complex history given that enslaved peoples in the United States were stripped of their cultural memory by centuries of barbaric practices by white slaveholders. Cookbooks from Virginia in the 1800s are rife with unacknowledged African-influenced recipes.

Mary Randolph's 1838 *The Virginia Housewife or Methodical Cook* is one of the earliest examples of the African influence on American tastes. Page 81 lists a dish that would be considered familiar enough at the time to warrant inclusion in a cookbook intended for 'beginning household managers'—gumbo. Mrs. Randolph notes that it

Women's Pavilion display at the 1876 Philadelphia Centennial Exposition.

is 'a West India dish,' but as 'gumbo' is a phonetic jumble of the word for okra in several Niger and Congolese regional languages—*ki ngombo*—we can definitively say it is an African dish. The recipe itself is nothing like modern gumbos: cook cleaned okra in a pan of water seasoned with salt and pepper until soft, then serve with a dollop of butter. What the inclusion of this recipe does illustrate is that American culture and cuisine from its earliest days was and is the great amalgamator, claiming what it wants and likes as its own with little thought of cultural ownership.

Modernity Means Now!

American cookbooks of the 20th century occupy a special place in our culinary and social history. They're a reflection of who a small group of corporations wanted us to be. The resulting fish-filled Jell-O® molds and SPAM® casseroles we find in these cookbooks did not miraculously appear sui generis out of the mind of a singular demented housewife. These were a product of the 20th century, the American Century, and how we got here is a result of luck, skill, and accident—the hallmarks of the American way of life.

The 20th century actually begins in 1876 in Philadelphia at the International Exhibition of Arts, Manufactures and Products of the Soil and Mine. The Exhibition was a World's Fair-style event organized to celebrate the 100th birthday of the United States. It soon lost its wordy name as most people referred to it as the Centennial Exhibition. Ten years in the making, its goal was to show the world the ingenuity of hard-working Americans and the unstoppable power and potential of the United States. Eight million people attended the Exhibition during its May opening through to its November closing. (That was 5% of the total United States population of 42 million.) The Exhibition paid particular attention to new inventions and agricultural improvements while a Women's Pavilion was erected to demonstrate the value of women in both the home and in the labor market. Wagner wrote the official opening march, and Emperor Dom Pedro of Brazil was on hand to open the festivities by switching on the giant Corliss steam engine that powered the entire grounds. The event, in no uncertain terms, was a worldwide phenomenon.

By bringing together the best and brightest of American science and manufacturing, the Exhibition created a space where inventors and businessmen met to collaborate on new ideas. In hindsight, it was the most incredible convergence of the American intelligentsia, aspirational middle classes, and entrepreneurs in United States history. Alexander Graham Bell introduced his new invention, the telephone. Thomas Edison was there with his telegraph machine. Otis brought his elevator, Remington brought their newly refined typewriter (the model with the QWERTY keyboard), and Nikolaus Otto's prototype internal combustion engine enthralled and terrified attendees. In the Women's Pavilion, the focus was on tools to make the manual labor of running a household easier and less time-consuming, creating more hours for leisure. There was a prototype dishwashing machine, various sewing and darning machines, the first removable handle iron, and importantly, the Reliance Cook Stove. The Reliance was the first freestanding oven/stove combination to use both wood and coal as fuel and valves to control and direct heat.

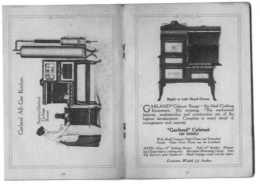

"Cupid in the Kitchen" /
Garland Stoves / 1910

In the agricultural building, attendees were introduced to Heinz Ketchup, Hires Root Beer, popped corn, and bananas. The Heinz brothers brought their new tomato sauce product after the earlier failure of a bottled horseradish sauce. Local Philadelphia pharmacist Dr. Charles Hires sold packets of his 'medicinal' herbal mix but won over millions by giving away free samples of the mixed Root Beer. Charles Fleischmann of Cincinnati followed Hires' lead and gave away samples of bread baked with his commercially produced yeast—the first of its kind. Fleischmann went from a struggling businessman to success in a matter of months. Before Fleischmann, bread baked at home relied on the housewife growing and keeping a 'starter' harvested from ambient wild yeasts. Imported bananas from Cuba were a sensation selling for a whopping ten cents each. (That's $1.75 in today's money and what would have been a full hour's wage in the 1870s.) So frenzied was the banana craze, guards were hired to protect the exhibit from thieves and vandals.

People talked. They wrote letters and postcards home. Journalists from around the world raved about the amazing new inventions and food at the Exhibition. These new ideas, machines, and food spread throughout the great and growing land, sparking the imagination of a people healing from a civil war and an economic depression. Genius is about having the right idea at the right time, and the post-Civil War period in the United States was an exciting time to be an entrepreneur or con-man, or an entrepreneurial con-man.

The Centennial Exhibition marked the beginning of a period of tumultuous growth resulting in a country reborn in modernity. In the 40 years from the closing of the Exhibition to 1910, the population of the country had doubled to nearly 80 million. Railroads embraced the steam-powered engines to build a comprehensive transportation system that joined east to west, opening up the western lands to occupation by just about anyone except the people who already lived there: Native Americans. Immigrants fueled the population boom, with approximately 25 million arriving, primarily from Europe, but smaller groups from Asia arrived from the Pacific to the new West. The new immigrants were not like the previous waves of wealthier Europeans coming to America to escape political or religious persecution. They were impoverished working classes left behind by the mechanization of European farming. The United States, as envisioned by mine operators, railroad magnates, cattle barons, and speculators, saw these next-wave pioneers as both the producers and consumers of their industries.

Banana tree display / 1876
Philadelphia Centennial Exposition

Exploitation of all resources, as interpreted by the Protestant principles of the ruling classes, drove growth-at-any-cost mentality. This exploitative ideology of the early capitalists is a thread that runs through American culture to this day. A country that had only recently and reluctantly abolished slavery based on the faulty science of 'who is a man' was not keen on allowing the indigenous culture and people to remain on valuable land. It was a time of untrammeled growth fueled by demobilization soldiers from both the Union and Confederacy; the U.S. Army soon followed to stabilize the Western frontier for economic expansion.

The promise of America was that of a place of unlimited opportunities for those willing to work hard. The French pavilion at the Centennial Exhibition displayed the now familiar torch-bearing arm of the Statue of Liberty as a preview of the final monument. Yet the experience of the millions of working-class immigrants betrayed the fact that class designations were still in place and that, though they didn't bear titles of nobility, the moneyed classes relied on dynastic alliances to build and expand their wealth. In contrast, modern economic theorists were developing ideas that blew apart the old aristocratic systems. The notion that a fair distribution of wealth among citizens would, in fact, create more wealth for the upper classes was far-reaching in effect. The concept that the poor could be turned from a burden to society to contributors became the animating myth of the United States. Bootstrappers and hard workers heeded the call of "Go West, young man." It was the birth of consumer culture.

A Great Awakening

I t was during the mid-1800s Industrial Age boom that the United States experienced a fervent spiritual revival. Called The Second Great Awakening, this charismatic Pentecostal revivalist movement touched all classes and denominations. Salvation was still personal but added a homey element—that heaven could not only be created on Earth but was an idealized version of the universe with chickens in every pot and eternal summer days. But to attain this new heaven, one must do more than believe and live a godly life; the charge of the 'saved' was to spread that message of salvation to every single person—especially those of God's creatures who lived in a primitive 'native' life, unknowing of the Protestant God. This new evangelical mission fit nicely into the American worldview codified in the Monroe Doctrine: God had given the Western Hemisphere to the white Americans to settle, save, and rule as they saw fit.

This revivalist spirit, though often associated with poor and rural Americans, was not limited to them. The established families of New England (the famous 400 Families of New York City and the Boston Brahmins) had long cultivated a culture of benevolent superiority. In this perspective, the immigrant poor and native peoples couldn't help but be filthy, lazy heathens as they have yet to know Jesus Christ. This version of revivalism took the form of missionary expeditions to bring religion, education, and modern industry to the western lands. In their patriarchal superiority, they believed that commerce and God would solve the nation's growing problems of crime and poverty by creating jobs that occupied idle hands. That the business made money for the evangelists was another way that God showed his approval for their mission.

In Boston, the oldest of the American puritanical Calvinist denominations, the Congregationalist Church recruited the educated students of Harvard and Wellesley to take up the 'good work' of spreading the Lord's message to the far-scattered heathens of the American West, Caribbean, and Central America. Those who could not travel to actual frontiers found their calling in writing. That they were also the children of the leading business and industrialist families helped both fund and fuel their missionary zeal. Women, more limited than men by the cultural restrictions imposed on them, were the most successful authorial proselytizers. Many authors wove their ecstatic vision into novels that were thinly veiled moralistic tracts (Louisa May Alcott's *Little Women* is the most famous), in addition to the traditional household manuals and cookbooks.

International Exhibition, 1876.

2025-COLOSSAL HAND AND TORCH "LIBERTY"

Statue of Liberty, torch arm, display at the 1876 Philadelphia Centennial Exposition.

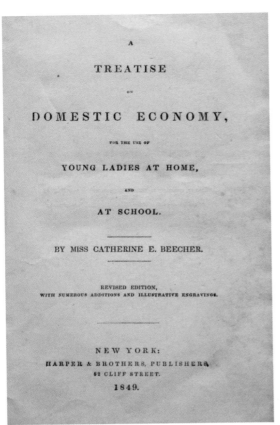

Catherine Beecher / *A Treatise on Domestic Economy, For the Use of Young Ladies at Home, and At School* / 1849

Catherine Beecher was an unmarried daughter of New York minister Lyman Beecher, and sister to abolitionist author Harriet Beecher Stowe. She took up the cause of women's education and founded schools in Connecticut and New York for poor girls using her, at that time, progressive curricula of mathematics and reading, as well as the Puritan 'moral philosophy.' She wrote textbooks that instructed women on how to keep a 'godly' home that included healthy cooking and dedicated cleanliness. She moved with her father to Cincinnati in the 1830s, where she set up a school to train teachers heading further west to the unknown frontier. She said, "Woman's great mission is to train immature, weak, and ignorant creatures to obey the laws of God; the physical, the intellectual, the social, and the moral." Beecher trained hundreds of women as teachers who were then sent to teach in the expanding West. Her model of 'homekeeping,' which was the foundation of education, informed both cookbooks and later cooking schools for the next 75 years.

Through their writing and teaching, Beecher and her zealous compatriots both defined and tried to reform the ideal for an American woman. She was someone who obeyed God and her husband while she worked to raise children who would become contributors to society. A critical piece of becoming that ideal woman was cooking food that was nutritious and American. For immigrants, this meant shunning the methods and recipes from the 'old country' and embracing the cuisine developed by a growing army of experts informed by science and given an appearance of authority by the dominant religious leaders.

"The Settlement" Cook Book (The Way to A Man's Heart), published in 1901, is one of the most famous examples of a cookbook that advertises an idealized lifestyle. Lizzie Black Kander's cookbook was explicitly written for the Milwaukee Jewish Mission, a group founded by the wealthier and well-established Milwaukee Jewish community to assist large groups of Jewish immigrants from Eastern Europe. The primary goal of the cookbook was to support immigrant women to assimilate into American life quickly, a life defined by the dominant Puritan-influenced Yankee pioneers and far from the agrarian lifestyle of the European villages. The earliest edition included recipes that 'Americanized' traditional Ashkenazi foods and tips for American-style housekeeping in the same tradition of Catherine Beecher's domestic manuals.

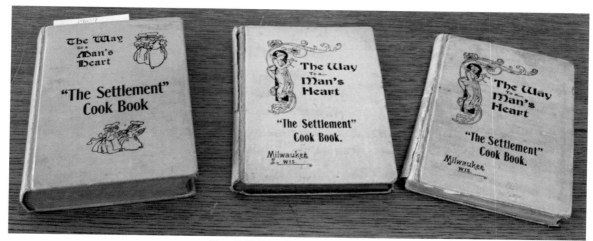

First (1901) and second (1903), editions of "The Settlement" Cook Book /
The Way to a Man's Heart by Lizzie Black Kander

Core to the American identity is the belief that anyone from any background with little education and less capital can work and will themselves into a success. Assimilation is (and was) the word often attributed to immigrant success. Being American meant adopting the foods of the new country while rejecting the old. In today's culinary world, 'fusion' cuisines that blend multiple cultural and regional influences are considered, well, ordinary. But for an Italian, Greek, and Jewish immigrants in the late 1800s, the kitchen smells of foods from home caused the established white Protestant upper classes to judge them harshly. Building a familiar American cuisine would sell more products to everyone. Yet fostering a national identity on conventional foods and the myth of hard work masks the multigenerational network of families that are the gatekeepers to American success.

Where Amelia Simmons' cookbook reflected the changes of an emerging multicultural society, the descendants of the founding Puritans and plantation-owning English gentry who still ruled the Atlantic coast cities changed tactics. They embraced the evangelical revival and the new industrial age as the perfect tools to advance the new American colonialism. At the same time, women were growing weary of the amount of physical, mental, and emotional labor required to live up to the ideal moral woman. Time-saving tools and machines coupled with a new sense of empowerment helped drive this women-led mission for educating and improving the lives of the poor and immigrant families. In Abby Diaz's 1881 treatise *A Domestic Problem* she begins by summarizing the chores of the average American housewife:

> "It certainly cannot be called trivial to enumerate the duties to which woman consecrates so large a portion of her life, especially when we remember that into each and all of these duties she has to carry her mind. Where woman's mind must go, man's mind, should not members scorn to follow. So let us make the attempt, and we need not stand upon the order of our counting, but begin anywhere.

Setting tables; clearing them off; keeping lamps or gas-fixtures in order; polishing stoves, knives, silverware, tinware, faucets, knobs, &c.; washing and wiping dishes; taking care of food left at meals; sweeping, including the grand Friday sweep, the limited daily sweep, and the oft-recurring dust-pan sweep; cleaning paint; washing looking-glasses, windows, window-curtains; canning and preserving fruit; making sauces and jellies, and "catchups" and pickles; making and baking bread, cake, pies, puddings; cooking meats and vegetables; keeping in nice order beds, bedding, and bedchambers; arranging furniture, dusting, and "picking up"; setting forth, at their due times and in due order, the three meals; washing the clothes; ironing, including doing up shirts and other "starched things"; taking care of the baby, night and day; washing and dressing children, and regulating their behavior, and making or getting made, their clothing, and seeing that the same is in good repair, in good taste, spotless from dirt, and suited both to the weather and the occasion; doing for herself what her own personal needs require; arranging flowers; entertaining company; nursing the sick; "letting down" and "letting out" to suit the growing ones; patching, darning, knitting, crocheting, braiding, quilting, — but let us remember the warning of the old saying, and forbear in time. This, however, is only a general enumeration. This is counting the stars by constellations."

Diaz's complaints are a rarely heard perspective. It was part and parcel of the modern American woman's identity to joyfully accept the gift of homemaking as her natural role and ultimate purpose. The tension between loving one's work while finding a way to make it easier is soon discovered by marketers as the exact space modern products and cookbooks can occupy.

The other drastic change in the United States in the late 1800s was the nature of work itself. Industrialization built cities and took families away from subsistence farming and into the towns where factories churned out new machines. Mechanization created tools to reduce household workloads and eliminated the need for an army of servants to do the repetitive drudge work required to maintain a household. (The endless hunger for invention also birthed the bastard child of this mechanical frenzy—useless gadgetry.) By the 1876 Centennial Exhibition, women in the cities of the eastern United States were less chattel and more members of the working and middle classes—their families earning enough to attain a higher quality of life, yet not wealthy enough to sustain a grand manner and the household servants required to maintain it.

With so many of the jobs traditionally held by self-sufficient farmers and laborers eliminated, the poor and working classes had the option of finding jobs in the new factories or trying their luck in the unsettled West. Millions of immigrants and internal migrants began the slow trickle westward. In two hundred years, the United States had grown from a colony of isolated agrarian communities and sizable coastal trading cities into a unified country with a distinct identity. It's about to get its own cuisine.

Armour Meat packing plant Chicago / 1910

Clean Eating

While Europe was fighting geopolitical wars during the late 1800s, the United States was in the midst of a battle between science and commerce. The European revolutions sent displaced scholars to universities in the new agriculture-focused land-grant universities in the Midwest and West. Their research invigorated American students and scientists who discovered new insights into the cause of livestock diseases and plant blights on a near-daily basis. The overarching discovery: Germs transmitted via foods cause diseases. It may seem like a given today, but without scientific proof, there was no basis for rule-making in the food industry. And worse, without a consensus of the citizenry, there was no impetus for legislators to take action.

The newly mechanized food processing industry adopted these scientific discoveries well before the public did, but used them for the not-so-altruistic goal of selling more canned and processed foods. The 40 years between the end of the American Civil War and the passage of the Clean Food & Drug Act in 1906 saw both brilliant advances in science and technology and gut-curdling misdeeds by the food and drug industries. Until German scientists in the early 20th century learned to synthesize active drug components, all drugs were plant-based. At that time, there wasn't much difference between grown and cultivated substances that one ingested.

Food contamination, still a problem today as evidenced by news reports, was worse 150 years ago. Milk fever, typhoid fever, dysentery, salmonella, ergot, and botulism outbreaks were a common occurrence. Unsanitary food handling spread germs while a lack of knowledge of how pathogens moved made every meal fraught with danger. Poor and working-class cooks combated this (whether they knew it or not) by boiling foods into stews and porridges, the higher temperatures killing most pathogens. Food-borne illnesses struck middle and upper classes as they indulged in the fashionable Anglo/French-style cuisine of the day which consisted of lightly cooked and raw items—the perfect vectors for pathogens.

The working poor were not entirely immune. They suffered large-scale typhoid outbreaks due to contaminated water and shared cooking spaces in overcrowded cities. The poor were also most often the victims of adulterated foods. We are appalled when we read of stories today of a rogue worker at the actual sausage factory deliberately adding metal pieces to the meats, but in the overcrowded cities of the 1880s–1900s adulterated meats were all too common. In rural and small towns, the local butcher was a respected member of the community. His business relied on the trust-based relationship with his neighbors that his products were fresh and free from contaminants. The urban poor relied on a purveyor with no connection to his customers. Meat production (of all types) consolidated into large companies and the consumer-producer relationship was severed. There are suitably horrific stories of individual butchers passing off everything from rats to human flesh as salable meats to unsuspecting consumers, but as the meatpacking industry grew from a local to regional, to national, to international business, it was guilty of its own excesses.

Where Grim Death Daily Lurks

DISEASE

TAINTED MILK

The topic of safeguarding young children is always acceptable to the editor.

J Campbell Cory cartoon / 1911

Foods were processed in filthy conditions without basic worker hygiene. Companies used inedible fillers and chemicals to extract more value from the food product, consumers be damned. Throughout the country, stories both horrifically true and comically exaggerated littered the *New York Times* and the local tabloids. Milk was watered and filled with chalk powder. Lead, dirt, and sand were all common additives before laws and science could determine the nature of the fraud. Even today, newspapers report of honey that is mostly corn syrup, olive oil that contains only a small percentage of olives, and fish mislabeled to attract higher market prices. Historically, the exposures of the egregious violations of the meatpacking industry were a catalyst that finally brought about change.

1900s Chicago, as famously described by poet Carl Sandburg in the first line of his poem 'Chicago,' was the "Hog-butcher for the world." The local butcher had wholly given way to the consolidated meatpackers—the four most significant in the

Chicago Stockyards / 1900

world called Chicago home—Swift, Armour, Morris, and National Packing. These companies, using the same monopolistic strategies as other robber barons of the era, bought out smaller slaughterhouses until they controlled 90% of the total meat markets in the United States, allowing them to set the prices for cattle, hogs, feed growers, consumers, and workers.

Slaughterhouse work is as dangerous now as it was then—the Henry Ford assembly line methodology adopted by meatpackers focused on speed. In creating the so-called 'disassembly line,' a job at the packing house was no longer a skilled position. It required a worker to do a single action numerous times. Filling those jobs were immigrants primarily from Eastern Europe. Children as young as 14 worked on the sausage-making lines, their small hands more adept at completing the work. Laborers made about ten cents an hour and worked 12 hours a day, six days a week.

The conditions were, as one can imagine in an abattoir, filled with blood, excrement and animal parts. There was zero initiative for hygienic practices as workers were punished for slowing down the disassembly line. In fact, the fastest workers were elevated to 'pacesetters' that were paid a higher wage to keep momentum and force other workers to move even faster. Profit was master, and diseased livestock were butchered along with healthy ones. The brutal pace and deplorable conditions fostered an environment where vermin and disease were rampant. These meats were then sold as 'fresh' to local markets while the remainder was salted, pickled, and canned and sold throughout the country.

". . . and when they were fished out, there was never enough of them left to be worth exhibiting,--sometimes they would be overlooked for days, till all but the bones of them had gone out to the world as Durham's Pure Leaf Lard!" — *The Jungle* by Upton Sinclair (1906), describing the fate of men who fell into rendering vats.

First instance of Upton Sinclair's *The Jungle* as a serial in *Appeal to Reason newspaper* / 1905

Sinclair's *The Jungle* was a literary sensation and became the tipping point of 30 years of investigative reportage about the state of the meatpacking, food processing, and drug industries. Newspapers shared the latest in scientific research about disease pathologies alongside reports of the social ills affecting poor and working-class people. A growing progressive movement, fueled both by science and anti-classist political ideas put forward by European philosophers and American thinkers, began calling for reforms to how the federal government would advocate for its citizens. These progressives believed that the notion of state-level regulation wouldn't force a change in the meatpackers' behavior—federal oversight was needed.

Revolution indeed was in the air. Further abroad, the French, British, Germans, Russians, and Spanish were fighting battles in their colonially controlled areas as well as internal skirmishes informed by new Socialist ideas of equality and access to capital for workers. American workers organized into unions, and Socialist politicians were gaining control of local governments in the Midwest with a broader goal of nationalizing the meatpacking houses, as well as making civic reforms to improve the lives of workers. President Theodore Roosevelt, hardly a socialist but always a populist, felt that without changes to ensure both worker fairness and food safety, a massive revolt loomed.

Roosevelt chartered a special commission to investigate the instances described in *The Jungle* and mounting newspaper accounts. What they discovered was shocking—conditions were worse than anyone imagined. The Meat-Packing Act of 1906 was the first enacted law to regulate how livestock was handled in a slaughterhouse and institute sanitary rules and regular inspections and enforcement. It was the first in a series of laws that became the Food and Drug Safety Act. These laws legitimized food science and ushered in an era when the government strove to regulate and educate citizens about the foods they eat.

The Rise of
Home Economics

Purity. The conceptual idea of what was 'pure' and what was not has hovered at the edges of American society since the Puritans came to the continent with their brand of Protestantism. It was even baked into the name—Puritans. Waves of immigrants from Eastern (Jewish) and Southern European countries (Catholic) were considered a cultural threat to the status quo of American culture. Their foods represented their moral failings as people relished the taste of robust flavors and hearty fare. Science would become the tool used to stem the tide of this insurgency.

The discovery of what is now called the 'calorie,' a unit of measurement of the energy derived from food, and the classification of foods as fats, carbohydrates, and proteins led to new ideas about how Americans should eat and cook. 'Scientific Cooking' took the place of the religious-inspired and infused recipe books in the 1880s. 'Scientific Cooking' utilized the newest technologies of stoves, ovens, and food science to educate both middle-class ladies and their servants how to fulfill the nutritional requirements of their families.

Nutrition trumped taste. The cooking schools, begun in Boston, were rooted in the same Calvinist culture that had spurred the previous generations of missionaries to write their household manuals. The new twist was the addition of science. While researchers were making significant progress in understanding human digestive systems and the food that fueled it, they were also responsible for ridiculous theories that not only were taught as fact but resurface again and again in modern food trends.

Meals were considered an opportunity for a mother to teach her family discipline and hygiene through scientifically balanced foods that promoted proper digestion. Hygiene was the byword for all aspects of the good Christian home. In the fashionable women's magazines, the harshest criticism laid upon a woman was that she was 'unhygienic.' The word encompassed a bevy of sins: a filthy house, dirty and unmannered children, non-churchgoing, a husband who visited saloons, and the woman herself if she wasn't presentable for public display at all times. The magazines and cookbooks

"What's In Here?"

Necco Company
candy advertisement / 1912

Cooking Class at the Boston Cooking School / c. 1890s

published by the Cooking Schools were chockablock with vignettes of the horrors of spousal abandonment, venereal diseases, delinquent children, and public shaming visited upon the woman who does not follow the rules of modern scientific cooking and hygienic practices.

What was considered a proper 'scientific meal'? Proteins and carbohydrates were prevalent. Fresh vegetables and greens were believed to have no nutritional value so were to be avoided. Excessive fats and sugars were considered decadent and led to the general moral decline. A breakfast of cakes and donuts would undoubtedly overtax the digestive systems and lead to Mister not performing his best at work. Meals were planned to stimulate brain growth and fuel industrious work. How much food to eat was determined by the newly discovered caloric measurement system, and excesses led to the sin of gluttony.

There was a sharp line drawn between deriving pleasure from eating and stimulating appetite. Spices should only add enough 'piquancy' (the commonly used word of the day to denote spices beyond salt and pepper) to stimulate the palate. Vinegar and pickled foods often made an appearance in meal plans as an acceptable stimulant that didn't veer too far into the realm of flavor. Raw foods, especially vegetables, were deemed nutritionally devoid and must be cooked and sauced to be rendered palatable. The ubiquitous 'white sauce,' which one does not dare call a béchamel, was made of three ingredients—butter, flour, and milk. Cookbooks would use French cooking terms, but only as a fig leaf to denote 'fanciness'—fancy was a common word used to describe recipes of superior quality. The white sauce could be slightly altered with sugar to be used for fruit or dressed up with the addition of capers or parsley, but never any spices.

Stimulating the appetite fell to other senses. The 'scientific cooking' teachers made visual presentation the hallmark of a proper meal. They borrowed methods from the French and British aristocracy; teachers recommended cooking and cutting up vegetables and placing them into aspics with mayonnaise for visual appeal or constructing elaborate sculptures with food. They developed and encouraged visually themed dinners—an all-red meal for Valentine's Day or the famed all-white dinners of the Boston Cooking School.

Best Mayonnaise advertisement /
Best Foods / 1960

Magazines benefited from the advances of the mechanical innovations displayed at the Centennial Exhibition. Efficient printing presses and cheap paper began the magazine boom in the 1890s. Publishers capitalized on the popularity of the wave of 'scientific cooking' and cooking schools and launched *The Ladies' Home Journal* and *Good Housekeeping*. The magazines encouraged submissions from their readers and helped spread these new ideas of nutrition and presentation. If one could not attend a famed cooking school, an aspiring housewife could buy the sponsored cookbook and subscribe to the periodical. In the pages of the magazines the cooking school teachers were the 'experts,' the celebrity chefs of their day, dispensing advice and recipes alongside product recommendations supported by advertising. In the early 20th century, the imprimatur of a Fannie Farmer would sell millions of stoves or baking powder.

The notion of purity suffused cookbooks and magazines. As both a reaction to food safety scares and fear of immigrants, the cooking schools recommended all-white kitchens, white aprons and uniforms, and of course, white sauces on top of everything. The messaging was clear: cleanliness was next to godliness and whiteness was American.

The righteous battle fought by advocates of what was now called 'domestic science' were winning converts with the housewives of the middle classes, but their message was lost on the immigrant women working and raising a family in a single room on poverty wages. These women did not have the time or money to fuss with daily caloric recommendations and the nutritional values of different types of foods when keeping the howling wolf of hunger at bay took precedent. The cooking schools did not and could not understand why poor women did not attend their free classes on cleaning, home keeping, and cooking.

The newly arrived immigrant poor were seen as both a source of corruption to accepted American norms and as an opportunity to prove how people can be elevated and transformed by domestic science. Across the country, women's groups and their wealthy patrons focused their rehabilitative energies on remaking immigrants in their image through food. Major cities on the East Coast and in the industrial towns in the Midwest had a number of 'settlement houses' that served immigrant communities that focused on either neighborhood or ethnic background. The lady-wives of the beer barons and manufacturing titans provided the funding, as it was in the economic best interest of the entire community that clean, sober, and well-fed workers showed up on time for their shifts. The women of the households were taught to 'Americanize' their recipes and adopt the 'scientific cooking' methods.

Domestic scientists attempted to address immigrants and the poor as social issues to be conquered by education. As documented in early editions of the *Settlement Cookbook*, the focus was on recipes that provided the maximum nutrition from a meal at the lowest possible cost. Magazines and women's clubs took up this charge as well. Contests challenging women to develop the most visually appealing meals that were also low-cost and calorically nutritious ones were widespread throughout the country. Mothers were castigated in the pages of *Good Housekeeping* for wasting hard-earned monies on luxury food items, while young wives warned that inattention to both the food budget and their toilette jeopardized their dream of owning a home. A woman's place in American society hinged on whether she embodied the virtues extolled by domestic scientists and reinforced by the advertising-laden pages of women's magazines; the ideal American woman was thin and well-groomed, her house sparkling, her husband sober, and her children clean and well-mannered.

The movement had some successes but often more failures. Poor workers rebelled against the condescending tone and strictures of the do-gooders. The hardships of making a new life, often transitioning from rural to city and agricultural to industrial work proved complicated enough without having to stop speaking one's native language and give up familiar foods. Domestic scientists put their inability to assimilate as marks of lesser native intelligence and ill breeding. Eugenics was another 'science' that gained in popularity during this era and dovetailed into the domestic science perspective that rejection of a moral and authoritative education belied not a problem with the teacher but with the learner.

Accredited

Mrs. Ellen Richards was the leading domestic science lecturer and writer in the United States in the late 1890s. She held a vision of a future where all women of moderate intelligence could aspire and ascend to the middle classes, and that pathway was through the domestic science movement. Women, as keepers of the hearth and home, would be empowered to lead their families away from the slovenly habits of the old world and transcend their origins to become real Americans. Mrs. Richards lectured with a missionary's zeal. She barnstormed throughout the country speaking at women's clubs and YWCAs about the dark fate that our country faced unless we changed how we ate, and laid the solution solely on women. Women must take charge of their families by keeping a clean house headed by a Christian man who provided for his children. Any obstacle to that outcome must be removed. The domestic science movement had its apron strings firmly tied to the temperance movement and less so to the suffragette movements.

After a few faulty starts at organizing the growing number of domestic science experts into a national advocacy group, the first meeting of leaders took place in September 1899 in Lake Placid, New York. Over the next ten years, they would develop a classification system for domestic sciences and define the work of maintaining a household in academic and scientific terms. The traditional women's colleges of New England balked at including a 'domestic science' curriculum, as their focus was providing separate but equal education to women as men received at Harvard, Yale, Princeton, etc. But the expanding universities of the Midwest and West embraced the new domestic science as part and parcel of their agricultural programs. The land-grant universities were not sex-segregated and felt that 'home economics' was: boys grow the wheat and girls make it into bread. Like many science fields of the era, one had to balance the good with the bad. Domestic science created opportunities for women, but it also disseminated harmful gender constraints, racist ideas, and plain old bad science.

Domestic Science kitchen / University of Hawaii / 1910

The expanding field of domestic science opened up a career path for women when previously their only job was 'wife and mother.' Unmarried women could study and then teach home economics in local schools and universities, or embark on speaking tours or write books and generate income independent of fathers, brothers, or husbands. Miss Isabel Bevier, born in Ohio, discovered both love and aptitude for chemistry at Case Western University, then went to gain further applied chemistry knowledge at Harvard and MIT (though as a woman, she would not be conferred a degree). Bevier, an attendee of the Lake Placid conferences, moved to the wilds of Champaign-Urbana, Illinois and set up the first university Household Sciences department in 1900.

The multi-pronged drive toward Federal laws that helped pass the Food and Drug Safety Act in 1906 pushed forward the Smith-Lever Act in 1914. This Federal law codified and funded the work of state Farm Institutes and land-grant universities in a singular Cooperative Extension Service that would develop and coordinate the newest and best science-based information to the citizens. It became a bridge between the 50-year-old United States Department of Agriculture and the work of university agriculture departments and their domestic scientists. Scientific Cooking, Domestic Science, Home Economics: though the names had morphed over its 70-year journey, Home Economics was now a legitimately sanctioned and fully funded field of study. The Experts had arrived.

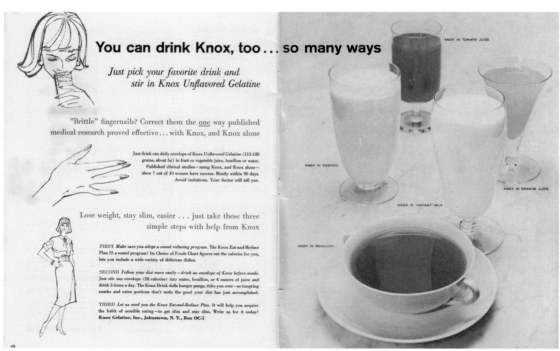

Knox Cookbook / "You can drink Knox too..." / 1962

Hunger Makes You
a Modern Girl

The domestic scientists of the 1920s all share a direct lineage from the Boston Cooking Schools, the previous generation of moralistic household manuals, and further back to the Calvinist teaching responsibilities of the Puritan Pilgrims. Ideals promulgated in the 1600s moved unchanged through American cultural history. Our concepts of what it was to be an American woman at the beginning of the modern age were, as they still are, defined by magazines, radio, and the new medium—movies. And like the previous generations, how you 'kept house' was the measuring stick to judge your success.

Home Economists delivered government-sanctioned messages of nutritional health focused on household efficiencies. Images of the ideal housewife in advertising showed a thin woman who ate her dinner only after her husband and children were adequately fed, the house cleaned, and the daily tasks of managing her household accomplished. Her pleasure was taken in knowing that her family was well served. But the physical challenge of housekeeping had changed. New tools, like gas stoves and refrigerators, standardized indoor plumbing and piped-in water, meant that less womanpower was needed to keep the hearth. It also meant that middle-class households who regularly employed a domestic staff to assist with tasks were no longer required. The modern, 20th-century woman was expected to manage it all until that time when she was rewarded with a passel of children, a larger house, and the hire of 'help.'

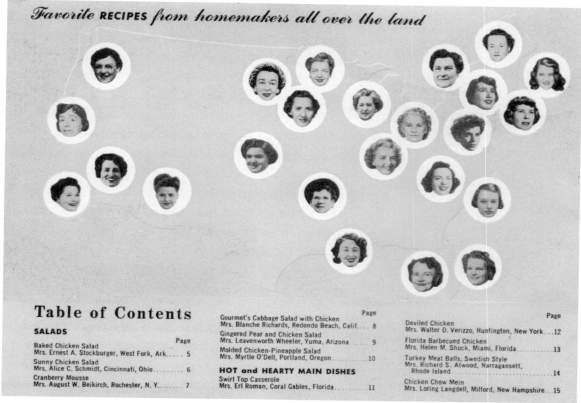

Favorite RECIPES *from homemakers all over the land*

Table of Contents

Swanson Company Cookbook, "Favorite recipes from homemakers all over the land" / 1938

As evidenced by the growing popularity of advice columns answered by legions of trained domestic scientists, the average American woman was struggling. Millions wrote asking advice from everything about feeding their families on limited budgets to how to please their husbands, all while keeping everything from the house to the dog spandy clean. After World War I, the women's empowerment movements crackled with new ideas about what women could do in a modern society. Some felt that more education to train women to be efficient helpmeets was the answer, while others felt empowerment lay in having more control over their bodies and lives. It was an era of mixed messages and agendas. Temperance agitators, suffragettes, birth-control advocates, and domestic scientists all worked to better the lives of women, sometimes together and often at cross purposes.

Many suffragettes felt that alcohol caused men to slack from the responsibilities of work and family, and garnered enough political will to enact alcohol prohibition laws. At the same time, other suffragettes worked to bring gynecological knowledge to working-class women, giving them access to modern birth control for the first time. Magazines and movies spread these new ideas to eager women. What message they heard depended on their age and class.

A younger woman of middle- and upper-class status, or one who wished to elevate her condition, was told by domestic scientists that thinness was a desirable trait. Only the lower and working classes possessed the robust and healthy body capable of the labor required of running a farm or working in a factory. Large bodies, freckled

Calorie Slim Recipes / 1967 /
The Pillsbury Company / Back cover

Kellogg's Corn Flakes /
Advertisement / 1908

by the sun, marked a woman as working-class as much as calloused hands and sturdy boots. Nutritional scientists of the 1920s agreed and recommended that women consume between 1000–1200 calories per day to attain and maintain sylph-like thinness.

Then, as now, women were encouraged to eat less, and their deprivation was held up as ideal. Why? Previously, plumpness held beauty value in times and places where food was scarce, while thinner body types came into fashion during bounty. The United States in the 1920s saw a chasm between wealth and poverty, and women who were rich embraced the new trend of shorter hemlines, dropped waists, and lowered necklines—a style that looks better on rail-thin bodies. The trend may have passed like the previous fads associated with wealth, but the drastic change from the corseted, voluptuous Gibson Girl to the waif flapper hinged on the combination of nutrition scientists and advertising.

Nutrition experts were exploring the possibilities within their new field with vigor. By the 1930s researchers shifted from an individual metabolism explanation for excess weight to a theory that body weight was solely tied to caloric intake. Insurance companies took note and funded even more studies that showed thinner people lived longer and required fewer benefit payouts. There were no government regulatory bodies nor professional association ethics standards in place to ride herd on the information put forth by doctors and researchers. Food processors saw this opportunity to fund studies on the benefits of their particular products.

There have been earlier health-based food fads. The Kellogg Brothers developed corn flakes and Rice Krispies at their sanitarium. Dr. Graham advanced graham crackers as a digestive acceptable to Seventh-Day Adventists. Both Kellogg and Graham were adherents to vegetarianism as practiced in the 19th century which was adopted as a temperance practice rooted in Puritanical Protestantism. Their diets were a vestige of the 'plain cooking' beliefs that easy-to-digest foods would temper both the mind and the body. The foods and diet plans were not based on actual science, but a combination of religious belief and 'common sense.'

Doctors eager to cash in and scientists searching for funding found deep pocketbooks in the emerging food processing industry. A few of the fad diets that recommended specific foods sound very familiar today. The 1930s Hollywood Eighteen-day

Diet consisted of 600 calories a day including one entire grapefruit. The California Citrus Growers Association happily promoted it with advertising in magazines. The diet reenters pop culture every generation or so but anyone trying it should be advised, it's not the grapefruit causing weight loss, it's the dangerous calorie restriction.

United Fruit perfected the messaging when it popularized the research of Dr. George Harop of Johns Hopkins University who developed a diet consisting of bananas and skimmed milk in 1934. United Fruit scoured the medical and nutritional research of the day to find the slimmest of correlations between health and bananas. It popularized a 1924 study by Dr. Sidney Haas that showed babies with digestive issues and failure to thrive were fully 'cured' when fed a banana diet. (Gluten intolerance and celiac disease had yet to be fully understood.) A diet of bananas indeed stopped children experiencing celiac symptoms. United Fruit touted this study as more than a 'cure' for celiac but a recommendation for all children in aid of digestion.

Another popular quack Depression-era nutrition theory was 'acidosis'—the idea that an excess of acid in your body causes not only weight gain but kidney and heart failure. Though legitimate research into the effect of ketones and epilepsy are proven, this fad, like so many, takes a smidge of verifiable science and turns it into a marketing tool. The acidosis fad reached fever pitch through radio programs, news accounts, and of course, medical doctors. The most egregious example of this run-amok system is when interested food producers funded the most famous nutrition researcher in the United States, Professor Elmer McCollum of Johns Hopkins. He researched acidosis, then supported the Sunkist brand in stating that highly acidic citrus fruits had an 'alkaline' effect on the stomach, which then received the endorsement from the federal government's Bureau of Home Economics. This method of 'advertising via endorsement' was successful for Sunkist and sales of oranges increased dramatically.

Vitamins were the next fad to hit the nutrition world. By the 1920s, the role of vitamins in food and how it affected a body was only beginning to be understood. Researchers could identify vitamins B, A, C, and K, but had a vague understanding as to how they could be measured and how much a body needed. Within a few years and for decades after, every food on the market was advertised as satisfying daily vitamin needs. Foods that were nearly devoid of any nutritional value were 'enriched' with vitamins that magically rendered them healthy. The American Home Economics Association depended on a consortium of food processors for funding, and endorsed their patrons' products in the press and to their member home economists and dieticians who educated consumers throughout the country. The circle of research funded by manufacturers who then, in turn, tout the findings in advertising is still successfully used today.

Enriched with vitamins. Packed with nutrition. Food processors, growers, and manufacturers were becoming savvier in convincing buyers that store-bought was better than homemade. Women's choices for feeding her family (but not herself) were becoming easier to manage thanks to pre-packaged foods. But corporations needed more than a simple magazine or newspaper advertisement to get their message out to consumers.

"A quart a day keeps the doctor away"/
The Sealtest Advisor / 1938

Psychological Manipulations

The specter of hucksterism has long tainted advertising; the snake oil peddler wrapped up in the carnival barker's gaudy coat. But between the advent of newly introduced psychological techniques in the 1920s and Vance Packard's exposé of the advertising industry, *The Hidden Persuaders,* in 1957, there reigned an 'anything goes' attitude. Advertising before the 1920s consisted of telling people the merits of your product. A typical ad in a newspaper or magazine would have an image of your product and name along with a slogan asking you to buy it. Sometimes drawings of pretty young women or cute babies were included to help draw the eye, but the presentation was straightforward with a clear message: Our Product Is Good.

Psychoanalysis was the European invention imported to America in the early 20th century that changed advertising forever. Dr. Sigmund Freud and a team of prominent Austrian doctors popularized the theory that the life of the mind is influenced by both seen and unseen forces, many of which go unnoticed in daily life. As a tool for understanding mental disease and aberrant behaviors, psychoanalysis

34

To keep a slender figure
No one can deny...

Reach for a LUCKY instead of a sweet

LUCKY STRIKE "IT'S TOASTED" CIGARETTES

"It's toasted"
No Throat Irritation-No Cough.

Edward Bernays' first advertisement for
Lucky Strike Cigarettes / 1923

became a fashionable pursuit for wealthy Europeans. It spread to the United States, as Freud trained thousands of doctors and acolytes in his techniques. Among those who were taught by Dr. Freud was his nephew, Edward Bernays. His place in food history is significant as he had the wholly original (and some would say unsavory) idea of using Freud's theories of unseen forces, subliminal messages, and psychological coercion to influence the behavior of consumers. It was Bernays' applied theories put into practice that created modern advertising.

Bernays believed that merely displaying your name and logo wasn't enough to convince people to buy a product. People needed motivation and a relationship with a product. His vision extended beyond advertisements, and he coined the phrase 'public relations' to describe the idea that a company, a product, a 'thing,' could exist as its own unique entity. He tested out early ideas in his work with the United States government during World War I. His projects included developing pro-U.S. propaganda aimed at Central and South America to keep up support for Allied war efforts. Later at the Versailles peace talks in 1918, he used the same techniques to ensure positive messaging about the Allied and specifically American actions at the negotiations. After his return from France he famously said: "There was one basic lesson I learned in the CPI (Committee for Public Information)—that efforts comparable to those applied by the CPI to affect the attitudes of the enemy, of neutrals, and people of this country could be applied with equal facility to peacetime pursuits. In other words, what could be done for a nation at war could be done for organizations and people in a nation at peace."

His first major commercial success was with the Liggett & Myers Company, a cigarette manufacturer. In the late 1920s cigarette sales were declining. Bernays realized that the majority of women did not smoke; culturally, it was considered unladylike, cheap, and dirty. Bernays sought to change public perception of women and smoking. There was never a direct advertisement telling women to smoke cigarettes, but a well-planned campaign of showing actresses and singers smoking. He worked with fashion magazine editors to promote the new modern beauty trend of 'thinness' while he coordinated with doctors to proclaim that smoking was a healthy way to curb one's appetite. Women began smoking in the millions and Bernays changed advertising forever.

Image from *New Orleans Creole Recipes* by Mary Moore Bremer / 1932

Racism Sells

During the post-Civil War era, African-American cooks were stripped of their authenticity and reduced to caricature. We see this in images used in advertising and branding in some form and fashion today. Aunt Jemima and Uncle Ben are rooted in the Jim Crow era. African-American women, deprived of their own families, were forced to act as nursemaids and caretakers to white families. Even after the official end of slavery, the social structures of the South treated dark-skinned people as less than human and without the right of citizenship. In portraying black women as the 'Mammy' caricature, white people continued to deny black women their autonomy, relegating them to a narrowly defined role as caretaker, nurturing the white people upon whom she depends for her livelihood.

Aunt Jemima is a typical 'Mammy' character who made her appearance in 1875 in a popular song ("Old Aunt Jemima") and was portrayed in the familiar caricature in blackface minstrel shows throughout the United States. It was the Davis Milling Company, who bought the recipe for a 'pancake mix' in 1890, who decided to adopt the popular minstrel character as their brand identity. They hired a formerly enslaved woman, Nancy Green, to portray 'Aunt Jemima' and she made her debut at the Chicago Exposition in 1893, making pancakes and posing in front of the 'world's largest flour barrel.' Aunt Jemima was a hit with the Northern crowds who had for the past 40 years indulged in a hazy-eyed view of Southern culture as an ideal of domesticity.

General Electric advertisement / 1935

Food advertising from the 1870s to the 1960s used these racist images to convey a distinct psychological message. The picture of Aunt Jemima sharing her cooking secrets with the harried white housewife was a message of subliminal enforcement of class. In the aspirational capitalism of the United States, even if a middle-class homemaker couldn't afford to hire a black servant, she could gain the advantage by using the products that shared the message of both superiority and Southern gentility.

Black men suffered a worse fate in modern advertising. Again, denying their humanity, black men were relegated to diametrically opposing caricatures of either stupid and obsequious servants needing the paternal white man to look out for them, or the subhuman animal with uncontrollable drives that required subduing. Born from the post-Civil War minstrel shows, the character of Uncle Tom, sarcastically named after the hero of Harriet Beecher Stowe's *Uncle Tom's Cabin*, was a black man with exaggerated features who personified the self-aware yet subservient caricature. We see Uncle Tom most often dressed in the uniform of a waiter or porter serving a visibly wealthier white person. Stepin Fetchit and Eddie "Rochester" Anderson achieved nationwide fame for their portrayals of Uncle Tom-style characters.

Frito Bandito / Frito-Lay mascot for its Fritos snack chip / 1967

Uncle Ben's Rice, though developed in England by a German scientist, was given the name and image of an elderly African-American man dressed in the bowtie and jacket of a waiter in 1946. The Mars Corporation has claimed that the product was named for a rice farmer named Ben, but there is zero proof to verify that story. Another minstrel show caricature, Rastus, graced the North Dakota-based Cream of Wheat product from its introduction in 1893. The Rastus stereotype of a kindly, dumb, yet happy-go-lucky man was made famous in the racist "Br'er Rabbit" children's stories and songs. In 1920, Cream of Wheat changed the illustrated Rastus caricature to the image of a Chicago-based chef, Frank White. Though Mr. White was a skilled chef, his picture conveyed the same lingering racist connotations. American advertisers used blatantly racist jokes and caricatured images not as a direct endorsement of a product, but as a method to reinforce stereotypes.

As the Civil Rights movement grew post-World War II, corporations using these images gave subtle makeovers to the caricatures and developed full personas transforming mascots into spokespeople. Aunt Jemima received a makeover in 1989, the 100th anniversary of the brand, changing her from the Mammy archetype by removing her headscarf and apron and lightening her skin tone into a composite of a middle-class, African-American housewife with the requisite pearl necklace.

Sugar Coated Rice Krinkles featuring
mascot "So-Hi" / General Foods
Corporation / 1965

Uncle Ben and Chef Frank White got facelifts and wardrobe updates, yet the racist undertones remain.

People of color suffered the most virulent and dehumanizing treatment in the hands of food advertisers, as any culture outside of the dominant white, Anglo-Saxon, Protestant society was deemed exotic. From the introduction of Miss Chiquita by the United Fruit Company in 1944 to the Frito Bandito in 1967 by the Frito-Lay Corporation, food manufacturers have used racially charged imagery and language to communicate a specific message to potential buyers. These caricatures, usually an illustrated cartoon, served as cultural shorthand to white consumers that negates fear of the unknown and renders the product safe.

In 1971, the Mexican Anti-Defamation League successfully sued Frito-Lay to stop using the Frito Bandito character. It marked the end of blatantly racist food advertising, yet corporations today still create insensitive and offensive food advertising, especially when their marketers are attempting to speak to a specific group. Conversations today are addressing the idea of 'food colonization' by both reclaiming natively grown foods and cooking techniques, and writing corrective histories that recognize the contributions of marginalized cooks and early food pioneers.

Modern Mad Men

Edward Bernays wasn't alone in adopting and adapting the new science for marketing. The legendary advertising mogul Walter J. Thompson began formulating product campaigns in the 1920s that were, as he described them, 'the psycho-seduction' of a consumer. He relied on the expertise of John Watson, who put forward the theory of 'behaviorism.' The theory that all actions are learned habits, when applied in advertising was subversive at the time: determine what people want, then give it to them. Soon all companies and advertisers were speaking directly to customers to discover their opinions about their products as well as their religious, political, and cultural beliefs to build consumer profiles. This led to insights that seem mundane today: consumers could be identified and segmented. A product was no longer a product in and of itself; it too became part of the advertising designed to appeal to a targeted group.

Food processors worked with marketing, public relations, and advertising experts to speak directly to the likes and habits of their customers. What kind of music do married women enjoy? Who was dad's favorite actor? Where did the family go on vacation? What kind of car did they own, would they like to own? All of this data helped marketers target their efforts to both likely buyers and, more importantly, preferred buyers. A dairy selling milk in a densely populated city projected a message of wholesome goodness with images of bucolic farms because research showed people bought more milk if they thought it was produced at a small, family-owned farm. Whether luxury-minded or homespun, soon all food products used design and copywriting to project desirability to the targeted group.

Procter & Gamble of Cincinnati were early pioneers of this style of marketing and advertising. The company founded in the 1830s began as a candle and soap maker taking advantage of the rendered fats as a byproduct of the pork processing plants that called Cincinnati home. (The Queen City also proudly called itself Porkopolis.) Tallow soaps were dense and brown, unlike the pastel-colored luxury olive oil-based soaps imported from France. Harley Procter charged his scientists to find a new fat that would make a lighter soap—thus was born Ivory Soap from a combination of hydrogenated palm and coconut oils. More experiments with different oils for saponification led to the discovery that hydrogenation (the chemical process of adding hydrogen to oil to make it solid) in some oils resulted in a lard-like substance. Procter & Gamble named the concoction Crisco and unleashed it onto the world in 1911.

Harvey Procter was lauded as a marketing genius for his forward thinking in both

Proctor & Gamble's Crisco /
Advertisement / 1936

Proctor & Gamble's Fluffo /
Advertisement / c. 1955

product development and marketing savvy. Crisco, a German-style abbreviation for 'crystalized cottonseed oil,' cost less to produce than animal-based lards. He began selling it as a healthier vegetable shortening. Crisco was packaged much as it is today, with its distinctive blue can and crisp red font with a flame dotting the 'I' (to denote its superiority for frying). It was designed to appeal to the middle-class housewife nurtured on scientific cooking and home economic ideals.

Crisco was a hit, but only with a particular class of shoppers. P&G understood that their vegetable shortening would be attractive to all buyers, but was aware of the cultural class divide in the United States. They learned from the debacle Schlitz Beer experienced in the 1940s when Schlitz attempted to grow their market by releasing an ad campaign aimed toward white-collar professionals who research showed preferred Miller Brewing's High Life lager ('the champagne of beers'). Schlitz's core demographic of working-class buyers felt betrayed by 'their' brand and sales dropped by nearly 30% in that year.

P&G's strategy was to sell the same product to a different audience under a different name. Thus Crisco became 'Fluffo' to a new consumer. Its golden color, thanks to a bit of yellow dye, assured users that it was an affordable substitute for the more costly butter when used for frying and baking. Fundamentally it was the same as Crisco except for the color and packaging—which harkened back to a down-home cooking style and a working-class consumer. The practice is now standard, and visitors to different parts of the country are often surprised when they encounter a familiar product with a different name.

Ketchup *is a* Vegetable

The success of Crisco also helped put to rest an ongoing ideological debate between food scientists, processors, and the government. What exactly can be called 'food'? The Pure Food & Drug Act of 1906 and the policies enacted in the ensuing years required a recipe-based system for labeling. It meant that for a manufacturer to call a food by a name, it had to hew closely to the recipe one would use when making it at home. For a jam to be called a jam, it must contain 50% fruit. Anything else was a fake and fraudulent under the law.

This method worked well for the United States, but for the Europeans during World War I who suffered food shortages and actual starvation edible alternatives were required. The German government challenged scientists and cooks to develop 'imitation' or ersatz foods that could be substituted. The entire semantical definition of what is a food was now turned on its head. 'Coffee' was made from ground walnut shells mixed with chicory, 'eggs' were made from ground cornmeal and potato, the concoctions passed off as ersatz became laughable. Proteins were the hardest to come by during the war years and gave rise to hair-raising tales of any and all animal proteins being sold and served to starving residents. A Berlin joke of the time went, "one didn't mind eating rat meat, but imitation rat was intolerable."

Food rationing eventually came to the United States, and the government encouraged citizens to embrace lesser quality meats and imitation foods as a way to support the war effort. The newly empowered home economists throughout the nation were set to the task of developing recipes that the average housewife could make at home. The word 'mock' was introduced into the culinary lexicon with the introduction of 'mock chicken legs' (a combination of pork and veal), 'mock turtle soup' (predominantly consumed by people who'd never eaten real turtle soup and wouldn't recognize that the chief ingredient of boiled calf's head stock tasted nothing like turtle), and 'mock lobster,' which perversely became more popular when renamed as 'Poor Man's Lobster' (halibut or cod).

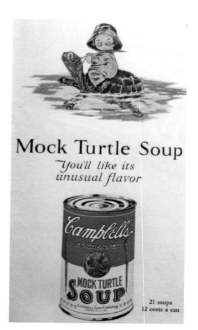

Mock Turtle Soup /
Magazine advertisement /
Campbell's Soup Company / 1928

Food processors developed canned meat protein products that were mostly salty fat but delivered the required calorie counts to fuel the soldiers fighting overseas. When the war ended, the glut of SPAM®, Treet, corned beef, Vienna Sausages, and canned tuna easily transferred to civilian shelves as de-mobbed soldiers and sailors developed a taste for the products. Not to be left to chance, the meatpackers launched a robust marketing campaign to teach homemakers how to cook with their newly returned husband's favorite canned meats. Even the young Soviet nation contributed to this glut of imitation foods giving the world fish sticks, which were a mock version of a traditional Russian dish of delicately minced and molded whitefish.

The cookbooks published by the government and food companies touted recipes that used substitute ingredients as both economical and patriotic. Many of the recipes included in the cookbooks that addressed the social needs of rationing of World Wars I and II and deprivations of the Great Depression were aspirational. There were dishes and cooking ideas that gained popularity, but as we find in modern cookbooks, many of the recipes are both laughable and unpalatable. The lasting effect was that the American society horrified by the idea of adulterated foods at the turn of the 19th century now embraced fake foods as the modern way.

Food scientists were quickly making discoveries about the individual components of food. Sugar was a carbohydrate made of amino acids that could be isolated and combined in new ways. Vitamins could be distilled, concentrated, and added to foods; now anything could be made healthy with fortification. Chemists synthesized the flavors of fruits, vegetables, and spices to be combined, boosted, and mixed in any way the market might want. A preservative, a nutrient, a color, a flavor—the secrets of food were now unlocked and gave birth to a whole new category of foods, or what was being marketed and sold as food. By the 1950s, the American menu landscape had moved from scarcity to abundance, and the food processing industry wanted people to eat. ★

Molded *Foods*

➤ What is gelatin? Make no mistake about it, Jell-O® and Knox (as well as smaller independent brands) are animal products. Collagen, the protein component of connective tissue, is isolated in a chemical process then dehydrated into a powdered form. Hides, hooves, snouts, and other discarded pieces are the main components of commercial gelatin but poultry and fish also gel when cooked properly. Since its first noted use in the late 14th century, gelatin has been used to preserve foods. The act of encasing a meat in a gelatin sarcophagus prevented air from reaching the food which delayed pathogenic infestation. The lime flavor came later.

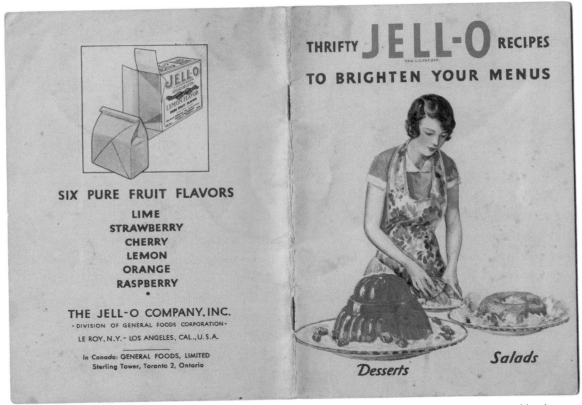

Thifty Jell-O® Recipes / 1931 / General Foods / Front and back cover

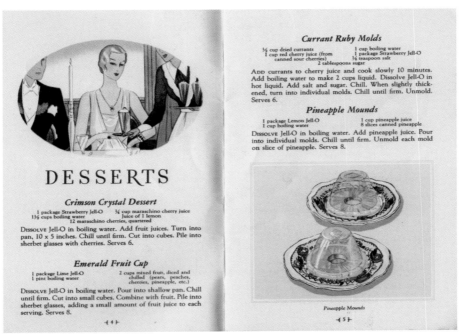

Thrifty Jell-O® Recipes / 1931 / Desserts / General Foods

Kate Smith for Jell-O® / 1947 Jell-O® advertisement / Kate Smith was an early celebrity endorser of Jell-O®. This ad shares Smith's personal recipes.

The Joys of Jell-O® / 1962 / Variety Vegetable Salad (celery and tomato in Lemon Jell-O®) / General Foods / Back Cover

The Joys of Jell-O® / 1962 / Sea Dream Salad (cucumber and onion in Lemon-Lime Jell-O®, fill with shrimp) & Vegetable Trio (carrots, cabbage, chives, and spinach in Celery Jell-O®) / General Foods

Jell-O® advertisement / c. 1950s / Savory Jell-O® flavors of tomato, Italian seasoning, celery, and mixed vegetable are introduced. This will be the zenith of the modern aspic-style salads. General Foods discontinued savory flavors in the early 1960s as food processors increased the amounts of sugar in foods and American tastes changed.

➤ Prior to Rose Knox applying for a patent for her method of isolating and dehydrating gelatin, most home cooks rendered their own gelatin as needed from calf or hog hooves. We look at these molded recipes with a modern revulsion, yet gelatin was a critical ingredient to the home cook. Beyond its oxygen reduction capability, it was used to thicken everything from broth to candy.

Knox Gelatine / 1936 / *Candies & Pies* / The Charles B. Knox Gelatin Company / Front cover

Knox Gelatine / 1936 / *Look! You Can Make 4 Different Dishes* / The Charles B. Knox Gelatin Company / Front cover

Every "On Camera" recipe belongs to one of the 5 types of gelatine dishes — each type is simply a variation on the easy basic gelatine mixture

Tomato Aspic is an example of Simple Gels made with **Unflavored Gelatine.** Simple Gels are really the same as the Basic Gelatine Mixture. A variety of liquids can be used and solid ingredients can be added for flavor and texture.

Pineapple Whip is an example of Unflavored Gelatine Whips. Whipping the chilled and partially set Basic Gelatine Mixture (until light and fluffy and double in volume) is the variation that is common to all recipes classified as Gelatine Whips.

Fruit Juice Snow is an example of Unflavored Gelatine Snows. All Snows have unbeaten egg whites added to the chilled and partially set Basic Gelatine Mixture. This mixture is then beaten until light and fluffy.

Lemon Chiffon Pie is an example of Unflavored Gelatine Chiffons. Chiffons vary from the Basic Gelatine Mixture in two simple ways: (1) egg yolks are added to the Basic Gelatine Mixture and it is then cooked. (2) This mixture, chilled and partially set, is then folded into beaten egg whites.

Bavarian Cream and Chicken Mousse are examples of Unflavored Gelatine Whipped Cream Mixtures. Whipped Cream Mixtures vary from the Basic Gelatine Mixture in just one simple way; whipped cream (and a solid ingredient such as chicken when called for) is folded into the chilled and partially set Basic Gelatine Mixture. In addition eggs are sometimes added as in Bavarian Cream.

UNMOLDING GELATINE DISHES

1. Dip mold in warm water (not hot) to depth of gelatine.

2. Loosen around edge with the tip of a paring knife.

3. Place serving dish on top of mold and turn upside down. Shake, holding serving dish tightly to the mold. If gelatine does not unmold readily, repeat.

3

Knox On Camera Recipes: A Completely New Guide to Gel Cookery / 1960 / The Charles B. Knox Gelatin Company / Explanation of the five types of gelatine dishes.

MACARONI LOAF
(Recipe on page 37)

ROYAL GELATIN SALADS AND ENTREES

MACARONI LOAF

1 package Royal Salad Gelatin (Aspic)
1 cup boiling water
¾ cup cold water
⅔ cup Russian Dressing
1 cup cooked elbow macaroni
⅔ cup chopped white cabbage
2 tablespoons minced pimiento
2 tablespoons minced green pepper

Dissolve Royal Salad Gelatin in boiling water; add cold water. Chill until it begins to thicken. Beat in Russian Dressing. Add remaining ingredients. Mould in loaf pan. Chill until firm. If desired, add few drops Worcestershire Sauce or onion juice. Serves 8.

CREOLE SALAD

1 package Royal Salad Gelatin (Aspic)
1 cup boiling water
1 cup tomato juice
2 tablespoons chopped onion
3 tablespoons chopped green pepper
2 tablespoons chopped pimiento
½ cup chopped cucumber
¼ cup chopped celery

Dissolve Royal Salad Gelatin in boiling water. Add tomato juice; chill until it begins to thicken. Add remaining ingredients; pour into mould and chill until firm. Serves 6.

CUCUMBER RELISH RING

1 package Royal Gelatin Dessert
    (lime flavor)
1 cup boiling water
⅓ cup cold water
2 tablespoons vinegar
¼ teaspoon salt
1 cup grated unpeeled cucumber

Dissolve Royal *Quick Setting* Gelatin in boiling water; add cold water, vinegar and salt. Chill until it begins to thicken; add grated cucumber. Pour into ring mould; chill until firm. Fill center with lobster, shrimp or flaked crabmeat salad. Serves 6 to 8.

TOMATO ASPIC RING WITH CABBAGE SALAD

1 package Royal Salad Gelatin (Aspic)
2 cups tomato juice
Cabbage Salad

Heat 1 cup of tomato juice to boiling. Pour over Royal Salad Gelatin and stir until dissolved. Add 1 cup of cold tomato juice.

Stir again. Pour into ring mould and chill until firm. Unmould and fill center with cabbage or mixed vegetable salad. Garnish with lettuce and mayonnaise. Serves 6.

WHITE FISH LOAF

1 package Royal Salad Gelatin (Aspic)
1 cup boiling water
1 cup cold water
2 tablespoons lemon juice
½ teaspoon salt
½ tablespoon finely chopped onion
1 pimiento, chopped
½ cup sliced radishes
1½ cups cooked, flaked white fish
    (haddock, halibut, etc.)

Dissolve Royal Salad Gelatin in boiling water; add cold water, lemon juice and seasonings. Chill until it begins to thicken, then add vegetables and fish. Pour into mould or loaf pan and chill until firm. Serve garnished with mayonnaise and sections of lemon. Serves 8.

PRESSED VEAL LOAF

1 package Royal Salad Gelatin (Aspic)
1¾ cups boiling water
¼ teaspoon salt
few grains pepper
few drops onion juice, if desired
    3 cups cooked veal, chopped or
        ground fine

Dissolve Royal Salad Gelatin in boiling water. Add salt, pepper and onion juice. Pack veal into lightly buttered loaf pan. Pour on dissolved gelatin. Chill until firm. Cut into slices to serve. Serves 10.

SALMON SALAD LOAF

1 package Royal Salad Gelatin (Aspic)
1 cup boiling water
½ teaspoon salt
¼ teaspoon paprika
1 tablespoon lemon juice
¾ cup cold water
¾ cup mayonnaise
1 cup salmon, flaked
½ cup celery, finely chopped
1 small green pepper, minced

Dissolve Royal Salad Gelatin in boiling water. Add salt, paprika, lemon juice and cold water. Chill until it begins to thicken, then gradually beat in mayonnaise. Fold in remaining ingredients and pour into loaf pan. Chill until firm. Unmould, cut in slices and serve on lettuce. Serves 8.

37

Royal Gelatin / 1936 / Macaroni Loaf (Russian dressing, elbow macaroni, cabbage, pimiento, and green pepper in Royal Salad Gelatin) / Nabisco

➤ Cooks continued to use gelatin as both a preservative and enhancement. It has no discernible flavor on its own but happily absorbs whatever flavors are introduced allowing it to be sweet or savory. Aspics are gelatins made with consommé or meat broth. French chefs in the early 18th century added cream to the meaty gelatins, called chaud-froid, translated as hot-cold or a hot food served cold. Any meat would and could be transformed into aspic. Victorian-era chefs took great pride in creating artistic presentations of these aspics, often fashioning the dish to represent its original form or sculpt them into elaborate architectural structures.

THE MIDWEST   **18s**

PERFECTION SALAD

McCall's Great American Recipe Card Collection

McCall's Great American Recipe Card Collection / Perfection Salad / 1973 / Perfection Salad made its first appearance in Knox Gelatin's Dainty Dishes published the 1930s. It has become the symbolic recipe of the excesses of molded gelatin salads.

Cranberry Heart Salad

(Illustrated below)

2 cups cranberries	½ cup chopped nuts
1 cup sugar	¾ cup diced
1 tablespoon gelatin	celery
½ cup cold water	Mazola Mayonnaise
Few grains salt	Dressing

Wash cranberries. Cover with cold water. Cook until tender. Add sugar. Cook 5 minutes. Soften gelatin in cold water. Add gelatin and salt to cranberries. Stir until dissolved. Chill until partly set. Add celery and nuts. Mix thoroughly. Pour into heart-shaped molds. Chill until firm. Unmold. Serve on crisp lettuce. Garnish with Mazola mayonnaise.

—*Household Magazine*

In the illustration white curly endive was used to suggest the lace paper of a valentine.

(A recipe for Mazola Mayonnaise is given on page 10.)

Three Fruit Salad Plate

6 lettuce leaves	½ cup Cream Mayonnaise
12 canned pineapple sticks	1 (3 oz.) package
1 cup orange, chopped	cream cheese
1 cup bananas, sliced	1 tablespoon cream
6 pecan halves	

Arrange lettuce leaves on salad platter; on each leaf place 2 pineapple sticks. Mix chopped oranges and bananas with Cream Mayonnaise. Place a heaping tablespoon of the mixture on pineapple sticks. Soften cheese with the cream and make into 6 balls, pressing a half pecan into center of each ball. Use these to garnish the salad. This makes 6 servings.

—*Pictorial Review-Delineator*

(A recipe for Cream Mayonnaise is given on page 10.)

Mazola Salad Bowl Recipes / 1938 / Cranberry Heart Salad (Cranberries, sugar, nuts, celery, and mayonnaise in gelatin) / Associated British Foods / This die-cut cookbook spared no expense to convey the quality of Mazola Salad Oil, which is used as an ingredient in every recipe.

Terrine of Garden Vegetables

Appetizers / 1982 / Terrine of Garden Vegetables (carrots, peas, green beans, spinach, and artichokes in gelatin) / *Bon Appetit* Magazine Publishing / Magazines published collections of recipes as separate cookbooks as an added revenue stream to entice both consumers and advertisers.

The Thatched Kitchen / 1972 / Ruby Borscht Salad (Dole pineapple, raspberry gelatin, shoestring beets, celery, dill, sour cream) / Castle & Cooke / Though published by Doubleday, a legitimate publisher, the copyright belongs to Castle & Cooke, the company that in 1972 was the owner of the Dole Pineapple brand.

Pineapple

➤ The Dole Company held a virtual monopoly on pineapple cultivation and processing. (Del Monte was a close second.) Dole excelled at creating a mystique that equated exoticism and Hawaii with pineapples, and the recipes featured in their cookbooks reflect marketing rather than actual culinary influence. After World War II, sailors and marines returning home from the Pacific theater brought back tales of Polynesian culture. Luaus and tiki bars became all the rage and for the mid-century housewife, adding pineapple to any dish made it exotic.

Hawaiian Pineapple as 100 Good Cooks Serve It / 1926 / Association of Hawaiian Pineapple Growers / Front and back cover

the pineapple cookbook

12 favorite recipes from the Dole kitchen

The Pineapple Cookbook / 1960 / Dole Company / Front cover

The Thatched Kitchen / 1972 / Castle & Cooke / Front cover

The Thatched Kitchen / 1972 / Crown of Lamb Royale / Castle & Cooke

➤ The New York World's Fair was an event showcasing the best of states, countries, and companies. The Hawaiian Big Five helped underwrite the spectacular Hawaiian Pavilion. The Dole Company sponsored this souvenir cookbook that featured the history of the company and popular recipes.

FIJI BEEF CHUNKS
(photo on opposite page)

Juicy meat cubes, tangy pineapple, crisp tender vegetables in richly accented brown sauce.

2½ pounds beef sirloin tip	½ cup sliced celery
1½ teaspoons garlic salt	½ cup sliced green pepper
1 teaspoon paprika	1 cup sliced onion
¼ cup cooking oil	2 large tomatoes
1 (13½-ounce) can pineapple chunks	1 tablespoon soy sauce
	3 tablespoons brown sugar
1 (10½-ounce) can beef broth	1 tablespoon cornstarch
¼ cup wine vinegar	½ cup water

Trim fat from meat; cut in 2-inch cubes. Sprinkle with garlic salt and paprika. Brown in hot oil. Drain off fat. Add syrup from pineapple, beef broth and half of vinegar. Cover; simmer 1½ hours. Add celery and pepper; cook 5 minutes. Add onion; cook 5 minutes more. Stir in tomatoes cut in wedges and pineapple chunks. Blend soy sauce, brown sugar, cornstarch, water and rest of vinegar; stir into sauce. Simmer until thickened. Makes 4 servings.

TONGA SPARERIBS

A glaze to glamorize ham and pork, too.

TONGA GLAZE: Heat to simmering 1 (8¾-ounce) can crushed pineapple, ⅓ cup **each** honey and pineapple juice, 3 tablespoons vinegar, 1 tablespoon **each** soy sauce and minced onion and 2 teaspoons ginger.

OVEN RIBS: Sprinkle 2 sides meaty spareribs (about 4 pounds) with salt and pepper. Arrange in single layer in shallow pan. Bake in hot oven (400 degrees F.) 30 to 40 minutes. Drain off fat. Lower heat to 325 degrees F. Bake ½ hour. Spoon on part of glaze. Continue baking 30 to 40 minutes longer, basting occasionally with glaze. Makes 4 servings.

CHARCOAL GRILLED RIBS: Select lean ribs. Use oven method up to point of draining off fat. Grill, basting with glaze, until ribs are tender.

✳ *Be lavish with gorgeous flowers and shiny green leaves to create an atmosphere of Polynesian splendor. If large, exotic blooms aren't available, fake ones may be just as lush and even more manageable. Sea shells and fish nets do much to accent the luau theme.*

3

Make Again Recipes Inspired by Canned Pineapple / 1964 / Fiji Beef Chunks & Tonga Spareribs / New York World's Fair Souvenir by Dole Pineapple

CALLIOPE PINEAPPLE SALAD BOWL
(photo on opposite page)

A circus of colors on lettuce bed. The dressing's delicious!

1 (1-pound 14-ounce) can
  pineapple slices
Finely shredded lettuce
1 (8-ounce) package cream
  cheese

¼ cup chopped Macadamia nuts
16 cherry tomatoes
8 deviled egg halves
  Rosy Chutney Dressing

Stack 2 drained pineapple slices in center of each salad bowl filled with finely shredded lettuce. Cut 4 (1-inch) squares from cream cheese; sprinkle with chopped nuts. Set one square on top of each pineapple stack. Make criss cross cut in top of each tomato. Soften remaining cream cheese and press through pastry tube into centers. Arrange 2 deviled egg halves and 4 tomatoes on each salad. Serve with dressing. Makes 4 servings.

ROSY CHUTNEY DRESSING: Blend thoroughly ½ cup salad oil, ¼ cup wine vinegar, 1 teaspoon **each** dry mustard and sugar, ½ teaspoon salt and 2 tablespoons **each** chili sauce and chopped chutney.

✳ *Salad Garnish: Thread pineapple chunks and ripe olives on toothpicks.*

SHERRY PINEAPPLE TOWER SALADS
(photo on opposite page)

*An elegant array of fruits in shimmering sherry flavored gelatin . . .
nippy with ginger.*

1 (1-pound 4½-ounce) can
  pineapple tidbits
  Hot water
1 (6-ounce) package lemon
  flavored gelatin
½ cup sherry
¼ cup lemon juice
⅛ teaspoon salt

1 (7-ounce) bottle lemon-
  lime carbonated beverage
½ cup thinly sliced celery
½ cup sliced strawberries
1 tablespoon finely chopped
  candied ginger
1 (1-pound 14-ounce) can
  pineapple slices

To syrup from pineapple tidbits add water to make 2 cups liquid. Combine with gelatin. Heat, stirring until dissolved. Take from heat. Add sherry, lemon juice and salt. Gently stir in carbonated beverage. Chill until mixture starts to thicken. Fold in drained pineapple tidbits, celery, strawberries and ginger. Spoon into 8 (5-ounce) molds. Chill until firm. Unmold each salad on drained pineapple slice. Serve with sour cream. Makes 8 servings.

14

*Make Again Recipes Inspired by Canned Pineapple / 1964 / Calliope Pineapple
Salad Bowl & Sherry Pineapple Tower Salads /
New York World's Fair Souvenir by Dole Pineapple*

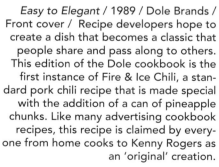

Easy to Elegant / 1989 / Dole Brands / Front cover / Recipe developers hope to create a dish that becomes a classic that people share and pass along to others. This edition of the Dole cookbook is the first instance of Fire & Ice Chili, a standard pork chili recipe that is made special with the addition of a can of pineapple chunks. Like many advertising cookbook recipes, this recipe is claimed by everyone from home cooks to Kenny Rogers as an 'original' creation.

Easy to Elegant / 1989 / Fire & Ice Chili / Dole Brands

Dole Pineapple Recipes / 2008 / Dole Brands / Front cover / The Dole Company continued to print cookbooks long after most companies stopped. This is a heavy cardboard covered, die-cut book that contains classic pineapple recipes.

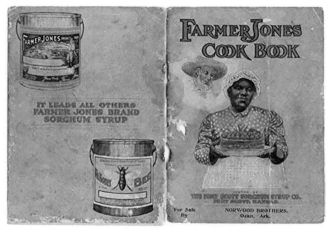

Farmer Jones Cookbook / 1914 / Fort Scott Sorghum Company, Kansas / Front and back cover

Tested Recipes for Cakes, Pastries, and Hot Breads / 1920 / Omega Flour Company, Chester, Illinois / Front cover

That's Not Racist,
That's our Brand

'Glory Be! Aunt Jemima Buckwheats...' / 1943 / Quaker Oats / Magazine advertisement / Cartoonist Dudley Fisher created this and a continuing series of illustrated ads for Aunt Jemima from 1943–1945.

'Pancake Days is Happy Days' /
1939 / Quaker Oats /
Magazine advertisement

Aunt Jemima's Magical Recipes /
1952 / Quaker Oats /
Front cover

'The flavor secret...' /
c. 1940s / Quaker Oats /
Magazine advertisement

Ah've always said, and now repea[t]
Ma health am due to CREAM O' WHE[AT]

Wallace for Cream of Wheat Co.

Copyright 1916 by C[.]

'Ah've always said...' / 1916 / Cream of Wheat / Diamond Mills /
Magazine advertisement

'First–Last and All the Time' /
1907 / Cream of Wheat /
Diamond Mills /
Magazine advertisement

'Rice was never like this before!' / 1950 /
Uncle Ben's Rice / Converted Rice, Inc. /
Magazine advertising / This ad is a
cross-promotion with SPAM®.

'Golly, Mis' Maria' / c. 1930s /
Maxwell House Coffee /
General Foods /
Magazine advertisement /
Maxwell House Coffee was the
primary sponsor of the Amos &
Andy radio program. Amos &
Andy were the character names
used by two white comedians
who performed in blackface and
whose humor was rooted
in minstrel-era racist stereotypes.

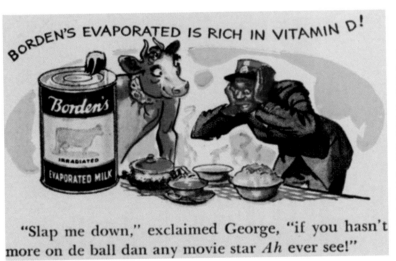

Borden's Evaporated Milk /
c. 1940s / Magazine advertisement /
Borden Company /
Evaporated and canned milk was a
scientific breakthrough that helped
provide calorie-dense milk to millions
of Americans. Unfortunately, the
good is shadowed by the racist ads
the company created in the 1940s.
An "Uncle Tom" character named
George was paired with Elsie the
Cow (Borden's mascot) to promote
the product in a narrative series
telling the story of Elsie traveling to
Hollywood to become
a movie star.

'Yassuh...' / 1938 /
Hires Root Beer / Charles E.
Hires Company / Magazine
advertisement / This ad is
an example of the "Uncle
Tom" stereotype showing
African-American men in
subservient roles to upper-
class white Americans.

He's making
Scampi alla
Parmigiana

Here's how with your own

fine Italian touch!

No doubt you already know what a savory partner Kraft Grated Parmesan is of soups, vegetables, salads, pasta. But now, see what it does for shrimp. For 4 servings, sauté 1 cup green pepper in ⅓ cup Kraft Italian Dressing. Combine 1 pound cooked shrimp (2½ cups) with mixture of 2 tablespoons flour and ¼ cup Kraft Grated Parmesan; add to green pepper and heat thoroughly. Top with a thick shower of Kraft Grated Parmesan Cheese (aged at least 14 months for finest flavor). Buon appetito!

TUNE IN KRAFT SUSPENSE THEATRE THURSDAY NIGHT NBC-TV

Fine Italian Touch / c.1970s / Grated Parmesan Cheese / Kraft Foods / An example of the stereotypical representation in marketing Italian-esque foods- a tubby, mustachioed chef.

Pillsbury Funny-Face Drink Mix / 1964 / Pillsbury Corporation / Packaging / The caricature of 'Injun Orange' and 'Chinese Cherry' were met with immediate censure when released as the growing civil rights movement took on racist ads. The Association of American Indian Affairs sued Pillsbury in 1966 but the company had already mandated changes to the branding in late 1965. 'Chinese Cherry' became 'Choo-Choo Cherry' and 'Injun Orange' morphed into 'Jolly Olly Orange' The product was discontinued in the early 1980s.

➤ Walk into any Chinese restaurant today and you'll be confronted by two menus—one features authentic regional dishes and the other Americanized Chinese creations. When Chinese immigrants came to the West Coast in the early 1900s they discovered that adapting traditional recipes to local ingredients and American tastes appealed to the growing population brought west by mining and railroad work.

Advertisers did little to differentiate between the varied cuisines of Asia, labeling foods as either 'Chinese' or 'Asian.' Once again, caricature mocking speech and otherness from the whitewashed ideal of the American family was the norm.

LaChoy / 1955 / LaChoy was founded in 1922 as a joint venture between Korean Dr. Ilyeong New and Detroit native Wally Smith. The company began selling canned mung beans to the emerging Asian populations in Detroit. Dr. New left the company in 1930 but LaChoy grew to introduce Americanized Chinese foods to consumers. The 'cook' mascot was used throughout the late 1940s though 1960s.

The Rice Council of America / 1967 / Magazine advertisement

Easy Surprise Meal is All Oriental / c. 1960s / Chun King Foods / La Choy competitor, Chun King was founded in the 1940s by Italian food manufacturer Jeno Paulucci. (He also invented frozen pizza rolls.) Paulucci, a first-generation Italian immigrant, used the racially charged imagery prevalent of the era in Chun King's marketing.

Tuna Foo Yung / c. 1960s / Chicken of the Sea / Magazine advertisement that was a part of an 'Around the World' campaign that used racist caricatures.

LaChoy / c. 1950s / Magazine advertisement / LaChoy created a white spokeswoman character "Beatrice Cooke" to help assure consumers that 'Chinese' food was acceptable for white, middle-class Americans.

The Ground Meat Cookbook / Culinary Arts Institute / 1955 / Chop Suey became an American dinner staple in the 1950s thanks to endless variations of this recipe. Nominally Chinese-inspired, the recipe illustrates how the Americanization of immigrant cuisine rendered the original dish foreign. The Culinary Arts Institute was based in Chicago and built a cookbook publishing empire using common recipes and the advertising cookbook format. The books are organized by theme and are distinctive by the singularly garish photos and frequent use of stereotypical illustrations.

Bananarama

➤ The evolution of the banana in the United States can be traced through the United Fruit Company cookbooks. The earliest editions, published in the early 1930s, divide the content into sections: how to store and eat bananas, the benefits of bananas, information about where bananas are grown, and finally, recipes.

By the 1970s, only the recipes are included in the books, showing that in the span of fifty years the banana moved from an exotic fruit to a common food.

The New Banana / 1931 / United Fruit Company / Front and back cover

Banana Notes

• • •

The digestibility of any fruit is largely a matter of ripeness. Bananas certainly are no exception. When ripe, or when cooked, no fruit is more digestible.

Like so many fruits, the banana has both a "cooking" stage and an "eating" stage.

COOKING STAGE—When the tips are green, cook bananas as a delicious vegetable, or keep a few days for ripening. Always ripen the bananas at room temperature; never place them in the icebox.

EATING STAGE—When all yellow, the banana is ready for immediate eating. The familiar brown flecks are additional signs of perfection—both in flavor and in the food value of the banana.

The distinctive flavor of bananas is pleasantly varied by their degree of ripeness—and by cooking.

To keep sliced or cubed bananas from turning dark until serving time, cover them with any canned or fresh fruit juice or sprinkle with lemon juice.

Ripe bananas may be whipped in a few minutes into the consistency of heavy cream, providing a basis for cake frosting, for milk drinks, pudding sauces and desserts.

Adding the beaten pulp of one ripe banana to each cup of mayonnaise makes a delicious dressing for fruit salad.

UNITED FRUIT COMPANY BANANAS
Distributed by FRUIT DISPATCH COMPANY
17 Battery Place, New York City

The New Banana / 1931 / United Fruit Company / Interior back cover

Luncheon—that meal which demands special planning—has brought banana dishes squarely into the spotlight. Bananas and bacon, for instance! Fried in deep fat or sautéed, bananas add a touch of genius to creamed chicken, veal bordered with rice or frizzled beef.

Eight

• FOR LUNCHEON AND DINNER •

Banana Waffles
2¾ cups pastry flour, or
2½ cups bread flour
4 teaspoons baking powder
1 teaspoon salt
2 tablespoons sugar
3 eggs
½ cup oil or melted shortening
1½ cups milk
1½ cups sliced bananas

Mix and sift the dry ingredients. Beat the eggs and stir in the oil or melted shortening. Add the milk, then the dry ingredients all at once. Beat until thoroughly mixed, stir in the bananas, and bake in hot waffle iron about five minutes.

Bananas with Bacon
6 bananas
¼ pound bacon
Roll half lengths of peeled bananas in strips of bacon. Secure with toothpick, if necessary. Broil under flame; or bake in oven-proof dish in a hot oven, 450° F., about fifteen minutes, or until bananas are tender and bacon is crisp. Baste at least once during the baking . . . Whole bananas may be wrapped in bacon and cooked in the same way.

Banana Fruit Cup
2 large bananas
3 tablespoons lemon juice
1 No. 2 can mixed fruits (or 2 cups sliced fresh fruit)
Peel and dice bananas. Drain off juice (if canned fruit is used), and cut fruit in small pieces and chill. Mix bananas, fruits and lemon juice and add the drained fruit juice. Serve in fruit cups and garnish with red cherry . . . Use either as fruit cup or dessert.

Banana Fritters
6 bananas
Powdered sugar
2 tablespoons lemon juice
Fritter batter
Peel bananas and cut in halves, first lengthwise, then crosswise. Sprinkle with powdered sugar. Dip in the fritter batter, and fry in deep hot fat, 395° F., until brown. Turn fritters frequently while cooking.

Fritter Batter
1½ cups flour
2 teaspoons baking powder
2 tablespoons powdered sugar
¼ teaspoon salt
⅔ cup milk
1 egg
Mix and sift dry ingredients. Combine milk and well beaten egg and add to dry ingredients, while beating constantly. The batter should be thick enough to entirely coat the fruit. If too thick, add more liquid; if too thin, add more flour.

Baked Bananas
Method I. Bake bananas in the skins on the rack of a moderate oven, 375° F., ten to fifteen minutes, or until dark in color and soft to the touch. Serve with the meat course in the skins; or peel carefully, sprinkle with powdered sugar and a few drops of lemon juice, and serve hot as a dessert.

Method II. Peel bananas. Arrange in shallow, oven-proof dish and sprinkle with lemon juice. Bake in moderate oven, 375° F., ten to twelve minutes, or until tender. Sprinkle with powdered sugar and serve hot.

UNLESS OTHERWISE STATED ALL RECIPES SERVE SIX.

Nine

The New Banana / 1931 / United Fruit Company / For Luncheon and Dinner

Bananas...How to Serve Them was published in early 1941 prior to the American entrance into World War II. It features full-color pictures and a caricature banana character that isn't quite Chiquita. A later 1941 pamphlet printed in two-color (instead of the expensive four-color) is fewer pages and smaller in size. United Fruit, like all companies during World War II, spun the rationing of raw materials earmarked for the war effort as a positive in their advertising. The postwar 1947 edition shows the fully realized Dik Browne-drawn Chiquita Banana in all her memorable outfits and poses.

Bananas...how to serve them / 1941 / United Fruit Company / Front and back cover

7 HAM BANANA ROLLS

Luncheon

Ham Banana Rolls
with Cheese Sauce
Mixed Vegetable Salad
Berries or Fruit
Cookies   Beverage

6 thin slices boiled ham
Prepared mustard

6 firm bananas, peeled
Cheese Sauce

Use all-yellow or slightly green-tipped bananas

Spread each slice of ham lightly with mustard. Wrap a slice of the prepared ham around each banana. Place into a buttered shallow baking pan and pour Cheese Sauce over bananas. Bake in a moderate oven (350° F.)

30 minutes, or until bananas are tender . . . easily pierced with a fork. Six servings.

•   •   •

Serve hot with Cheese Sauce from the pan poured over each roll.

CHEESE SAUCE

1½ tablespoons butter
1½ tablespoons flour

¾ cup milk
1½ cups grated American cheese

Melt butter, add flour and stir until smooth. Stir in milk slowly. Add cheese and cook, stirring constantly until sauce is smooth and thickened. Makes about 1 cup sauce.

Bananas...how to serve them / 1941 / Ham Banana Rolls / This is the first instance of the legendary Ham Banana Rolls. The 1931 edition features bacon-wrapped bananas, but now the recipe has evolved to swap the bacon for ham and add cheese.

Serve Bananas in "Latest Style" / 1940 / Fruit Dispatch Company / Fruit Dispatch Company was the distribution arm of United Fruit Company. They created and promoted branded cookbooks that featured a similar sexy banana illustration. United Fruit consolidated its branding under the familiar United Fruit name after World War II.

Bananas...how to serve them / 1941 / Banana Scallops and Glazed Bananas / United Fruit Company

Chiquita Banana's Recipe Book / 1947 /
United Fruit Company / Front cover /
Dik Browne's Chiquita Banana has
become the mascot of United Fruit
and a star in her own right.

Chiquita Banana's Recipe Book / 1947 / Baked Bananas, Baked Bananas in the Peel, and Ham Banana Rolls / United Fruit Company / These pages feature savory banana recipes inspired by the home economists at United Fruit taking inspiration from Caribbean cuisine by offering versions of baked bananas as a side dish. Ham banana rolls are also featured, a sign that the recipe received positive consumer feedback since its introduction in 1941.

Chiquita Banana's Recipe Book / 1947 / Salad Spectaculars / United Fruit Company / A combination of molded gelatin 'salads' and green salads. All feature the common ingredients of bananas and mayonnaise.

➤ The 1962 edition cover shows
a very modern styled photo
of bananas displayed in a
Victorian-era crystal banana
holder. It's a nod to the
1880s when bananas were
scarce and a luxury item.
One of the last editions of the
United Fruit cookbook was
published in 1974. The recipes
are particularly garish and
outlandish mirroring the craze
for 'gourmet' cooking inspired
by the growth of television
celebrity chefs.

UNITED FRUIT COMPANY

Pier 3, North River, New York 6, N. Y.

Chiquita Banana's Cookbook / 1962 / United Fruit Company / Front and back cover

The Chiquita Banana Cookbook / 1974 / United Fruit Company /
Front cover / The United Fruit name and brand had become tainted by increasing publicity about their history in Central America.
From worker mistreatment to fomenting coups, the company
name was poisoned—the marketing solution was to change the
brand name to its beloved mascot, Chiquita Banana.

BERKSHIRE SAUCE

1/2 cup red currant jelly
1/2 teaspoon prepared hot mustard
1/2 cup dry white wine
(Chablis or Dry Sauterne)
2 teaspoons cornstarch
1 teaspoon finely sliced orange peel

In a small skillet, blend jelly and mustard. Place over low heat and stir with wire whisk or fork until jelly is melted. Combine wine and cornstarch and stir into jelly. Continue to cook and stir until mixture boils and is thickened. Add orange peel. Serve hot over sautéed bananas. Makes 2/3 cup.

Suggestion: This is an eye catching and deliciously provocative vegetable to serve with baked ham, poultry or cold sliced meats of any variety.

46   *Berkshire Sauce*

The Chiquita Banana Cookbook / 1974 / United Fruit Company / Berkshire Sauce

ENTRÉES

Variations on familiar themes are found in these banana based entrées, many of them with a true South American tone. Bananas are plentiful south of the border and señoras long ago learned to combine their good flavor and nutrition with the main course as well as the salads and desserts. For something quite certain to be a new flavor combination to many, we recommend any one of these main-course suggestions as a unique enjoyment in eating. Many of them lend themselves to pleasant fireside suppers. Some are ideal for brunch. All of them are excellent food for the family as well as entertainment fare for friends.

Chicken Honduras   59

The Chiquita Banana Cookbook / 1974 / United Fruit Company / Chicken Honduras / Recipes in the 1974 cookbook are a nod to the trend for 'exotic' foods and cooking as a hobby done for enjoyment versus a necessary chore.

Food Councils

➤ Food councils were the brainchild of advertising executives. In setting up nonprofit advocacy groups that hired home economists to develop recipes and scientists to conduct beneficial research, the councils were able to establish themselves as 'subject experts.' With the advent of imported and processed foods in the 20th century, the food councils took a page from United Fruit and taught people how to eat. The resulting cookbooks issued by the councils are thinly veiled advertisements for the consortium of brands that fund the councils. The recipes included are some of the most memorable creations as the army of home economists diligently work to slip the highlighted ingredient into a dish.

Appetizing Recipes From Canned Foods / c. 1930s /
American Can Company / Front and back cover

A Parade of Brazil Nut Recipes / 1950 / Brazil Nut Association /
Front cover / Kernel Nut was the Brazil nut-shaped mascot of the
Brazil Nut Association and served as their symbol for a short time
from the late 1940s to the early 1950s.

FROM AMERICAN DAIRY ASSOCIATION TEST KITCHEN

Creative Cooking with Cottage Cheese / 1950 / American Dairy Association / Front and back cover / This publication left blank spaces in the design for customization from local producers and dairies. This example has the Lake to Lake logo on the cottage cheese container while other companies used the space after the word 'with' on the cover to add their name.

UP NORTH SALMON SUPPER

Loaf pan, 9x5x3-inch, <u>OR</u>   6-8 servings   Preheated 350° oven
Baking dish, 2-quart

2 cups (1-lb. can) red salmon,
   skin and bones removed
1 10-ounce package frozen peas
1½ cups cottage cheese
1 egg, slightly beaten
1 cup cracker crumbs
½ cup crushed oven-toasted rice cereal

1 cup shredded Cheddar cheese
3 tablespoons chopped green pepper
1 tablespoon chopped onion
1 tablespoon lemon juice
1/8 teaspoon pepper
Salt to taste

Drain salmon and partially cook peas in the salmon liquor. Mix together cottage cheese, egg, cracker and cereal crumbs, Cheddar cheese, green pepper, onion, lemon juice, pepper and salt. Add peas and salmon, broken into chunks. Spoon into pan or casserole and bake 45 minutes. Garnish with lemon wedges and parsley.

<u>Serving</u> <u>Suggestion</u>: A Lemon Almond Butter Sauce* adds a contrasting texture to the fluffy Salmon Supper.

*LEMON ALMOND BUTTER SAUCE
Yield: 1 cup

½ cup (1 stick) butter, melted
2 tablespoons lemon juice

½ cup blanched, slivered, toasted
   almonds

Mix together butter, lemon juice and almonds; heat to serve.

8

*Creative Cooking with Cottage Cheese /
1950 / Up North Salmon Supper /
American Dairy Association*

► Though simple in design and only suggesting simple recipes, the 1975 cookbook issued by the Pork Industry Group wins for its sense of humor. The P.I.G. created a series of humorous advertisements and branding campaigns to encourage eating pork as a healthy alternative to beef or chicken. The 'Promote Pork, Run Over A Chicken' campaign has been repurposed by other advertisers in many variations in the past 40 years.

Homemade Biscuit Mix

8 cups flour
¼ cup baking powder
4 teaspoons salt
1 cup lard for soft wheat flour or
   1½ cups lard for hard wheat flour

Sift together flour, baking powder and salt. Cut lard into flour with a fork or pastry blender until the mixture has a fine even crumb. Cover and store in refrigerator until ready to use. This mixture will keep at least a month in refrigerator. Yield: 10 cups biscuit mix.

To make biscuits, add ½ cup milk to 2 cups Homemade Biscuit Mix. Turn onto a lightly floured surface and knead gently for ½ minute. Pat or roll ½ inch thick and cut with a medium-size cutter, dipped in flour. Bake in a very hot oven (450°F.) 12 to 15 minutes or until brown. Yield: 10 to 12 biscuits.

Published by:

Pork Industry Group
36 South Wabash Ave.
National Live Stock & Meat Board
Chicago, Illinois 60603

475200

© 1975

Lard Makes it Better / 1975 / Homemade Biscuit Mix / Pork Industry Group (P.I.G.)

LARD Makes It Better Because...

1. Lard has superior shortening power to other fats.
2. Lard is easily workable over a wide range of temperatures.
3. Lard adds flavor and richness to foods, whether used as shortening or for frying.
4. Lard is 97 per cent digestible.
5. Lard supplies energy and certain other food factors necessary for growth and health.

Remember to Choose LARD for...

1. PASTRY that's tender and flaky.
2. BISCUITS, MUFFINS and CAKES of fine texture and feathery lightness.
3. COOKIES that are rich and delicious and store well.
4. BREADS with superior flavor of crumb and crust.
5. DEEP-FAT FRYING that provides a tempting golden brown crust.

Homemade Pastry Mix

7 cups flour
4 teaspoons salt
1¾ cups lard for soft wheat flour or
2 cups lard for hard wheat flour

Mix flour and salt well. Cut lard into flour mixture with a fork or pastry blender until crumbs are about the size of small peas. Cover and store in refrigerator until ready to use. This mixture will keep at least a month in refrigerator. Yield: 10 cups pastry mix.

Lard Makes it Better / 1975 / Homemade Pastry Mix / Pork Industry Group (P.I.G.) / In the 1970s, shortenings and oil-based fats had supplanted lard as the preferred cooking fat. In 1975, P.I.G. answers back with simple, homespun recipes.

The cookbooks issued by the Avocado Board in 1976 and the National Kraut Packers in 1970 are two of the finest examples of the over-the-top design, images, and recipes associated with the phenomenon. 'Put Some Kraut In Your Life' features pop art lettering and colors paired with traditional German-style dishes using sauerkraut.

The absolute triumph of the home economists is the development of the Sauerkraut Cake. The recipe's creator is lost to time, but it was her genius that made the connection that buttermilk-based cake recipes that used acidity to leaven could be made with sauerkraut. The kraut adds sourness and moistness to the batter while the chocolate and sugars become the prominent tastes. This cake still pops up on restaurant menus and in home kitchens. It's a favorite in Wisconsin, the largest sauerkraut manufacturer in the United States.

The Avocado Bravo / 1976 / California Avocado Advisory Board / Front cover

AVOCADOS ON THE HALF-SHELL . . . *with a filling of curried chicken . . . to serve as a luncheon or supper main course. For this creamed dish the avocados are peeled. This recipe is on page 20.*

The Avocado Bravo / 1976 / California Avocado Advisory Board / Avocados on the Half-Shell

The Avocado Bravo / 1976 / California Avocado Advisory Board / Avocado Ice Cream

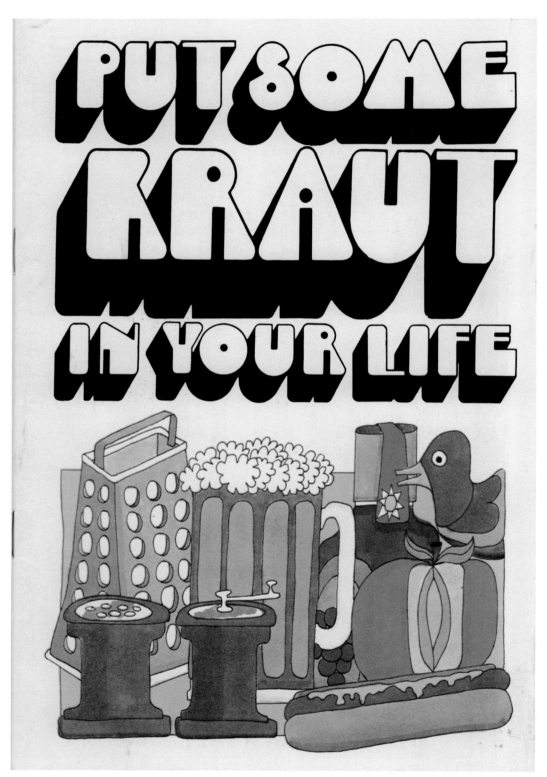

Put Some Kraut in Your Life / 1970 / National Kraut Packers Association / Front cover /
The dishes included are rooted in hearty central European cooking with an emphasis
on meats paired with sauerkraut excepting for the surprising chocolate cake recipe.

SUPER KRAUT

There's almost no limit to the uses for kraut. If you're not convinced now, we think the following delectable... if unexpected ... recipes will make a believer out of you. You'll probably have the greatest success with the more unconventional ones if you serve them first and divulge the "secret" ingredient later. The moist, tender chocolate cake or lemony ice cream containing kraut is sure to be pronounced super once tasted.

Kraut Conquers All ...
Chocolate Cake
(Makes two 8-inch squares or rounds)

This rich fudge cake has a coconut-like texture and the kraut keeps it wonderfully moist and fresh for several days. Top it with fluffy Mocha Whipped Cream or, for real chocolate lovers, Chocolate Cream Cheese Frosting.

⅔ cup butter or margarine
1½ cups sugar
3 eggs
1 teaspoon vanilla
½ cup unsweetened cocoa
2¼ cups sifted all-purpose flour
1 teaspoon each: baking powder,
   baking soda
¼ teaspoon salt
1 cup water
⅔ cup rinsed, drained and chopped
   sauerkraut

Thoroughly cream butter with sugar. Beat in eggs and vanilla. Sift together dry ingredients; add alternately with water to egg mixture. Stir in kraut. Turn into two greased and floured 8-inch square or round baking pans. Bake in 350° (moderate) oven 30 minutes, or until cake tests done. Fill and frost with Mocha Whipped Cream or Chocolate Cream Cheese Frosting, recipes given on the next page.

27

Put Some Kraut in Your Life / 1970 / National Kraut
Packers Association / Kraut Conquers All...Chocolate Cake

KRAUT & WURSTS

Ever since kraut was introduced to the frankfurter, kraut and wursts have been popular partners. Choose your favorite sausages . . . be they frankfurters, bratwurst, knockwurst, kielbasi or bologna . . . then whip up a casserole, a crown or a stew. Broil them or boil them or grill them outdoors. But however you treat them, kraut's the perfect embellishment to turn plain fare into posh.

Stout Hearted Kraut & Frankfurters
(Makes 4 to 6 servings)

Frankfurters with flare! This eye-appealing dish is sweet and sour in flavor and fits any budget.

3½ cups undrained sauerkraut
½ cup sliced celery
⅓ cup sliced onion
¼ cup butter or margarine
1 pound frankfurters, cut in ½-inch slices
1¾ cups water

¼ cup white vinegar
¾ cup sugar
1 beef bouillon cube
½ teaspoon salt
¼ teaspoon ginger
⅛ teaspoon pepper
1½ tablespoons cornstarch
Chopped canned pimiento, or sautéed chopped fresh red pepper (optional)

Drain kraut well and reserve ¼ cup of the liquid; set aside. In large saucepan or Dutch oven, sauté celery and onion in butter until crisp-tender. Remove with slotted spoon. In same pan brown frankfurters; remove. Add 1½ cups of the water, vinegar, sugar, bouillon cube, seasonings and reserved kraut liquid. Simmer, stirring until sugar and bouillon cube dissolve. Bring to boil; stir in cornstarch blended in remaining ¼ cup water. Boil ½ minute, stirring. Add kraut and stir in franks, celery and onion. Heat to serving temperature. Garnish with pimiento and serve with mashed potatoes.

15

Put Some Kraut in Your Life / 1970 / National Kraut Packers Association /
Stout Hearted Kraut & Frankfurters

Man-pleasing Recipes / 1971 / Rice Council of America /
Front and back covers

1½ pounds lean beef chuck, cut in cubes
2 teaspoons bottled browning sauce, optional
2 teaspoons vegetable oil
1 can (1 pound) tomatoes
½ cup Burgundy wine
1 beef bouillon cube
1½ teaspoons salt
½ teaspoon basil
¼ teaspoon garlic salt
¼ teaspoon pepper
1 small bay leaf
8 small white onions
8 young carrots, peeled and cut in quarters
2 tablespoons cornstarch
¼ cup water
Rice Verte*

Beef Burgundy Stew with Rice Verte
Guaranteed...man pleasin'.

Place meat in bowl. Sprinkle with bottled browning sauce and toss lightly until evenly coated. Brown in oil.

Add tomatoes, wine, bouillon cube, and seasonings. Cover and simmer for 45 minutes. Add onions and carrots. Cover and cook 45 minutes longer or until meat and vegetables are tender.

Blend cornstarch and water. Stir into stew mixture and cook, stirring frequently, until thickened. Remove bay leaf. Serve over Rice Verte*.

Makes 4 servings.

*Rice Verte
¼ cup finely chopped onion
2 tablespoons butter or margarine
3 cups hot cooked rice, cooked in beef broth
2 tablespoons minced parsley
Salt and pepper

Saute onion in butter until tender. Add rice and parsley; toss lightly. Season to taste with salt and pepper.

Man-pleasing Recipes / 1971 / Rice Council of America / Beef Burgundy Stew with Rice Verte

Substitutes!

➤ Procter & Gamble may have invented Crisco and Fluffo as lard substitutes, but they weren't the only makers selling consumers on the benefits of hydrogenated vegetable oils. P&G created a specialized and targeted marketing campaign to Jewish housewives touting the benefits of Crisco-you could use it exactly like lard, but because it was initially made from cottonseed oil, it was deemed pareve and pesadik or kosher for regular meals as well as Passover. There is some debate whether Crisco is actually food under Jewish dietary laws, but that didn't stop early marketers. An advertising slogan used in 1910–1920 quoted an unnamed Rabbi proclaiming, "The Hebrew Race has been waiting for 4,000 years for Crisco."

Creative Cooking Made Easy :
The Golden Fluffo Cookbook /
1956 / Fluffo / Procter & Gamble

The Art of Cooking and
Serving / 1934 / Crisco /
Procter & Gamble

Watch my hands in these 4 pictures /
c. 1930s / Procter & Gamble /
Magazine advertisement

Crisco Recipes for the Jewish Housewife /
1933 / Procter & Gamble /
Front and back cover

Planter's Passover Recipe Book / c. 1930s /
Planter's Edible Oil Company /
Front and back cover

Praise for the Cook / 1959 /
Crisco / Procter & Gamble

What Shall I Cook Today? / 1936 /
Spry Shortening / Lever Brothers / Front cover

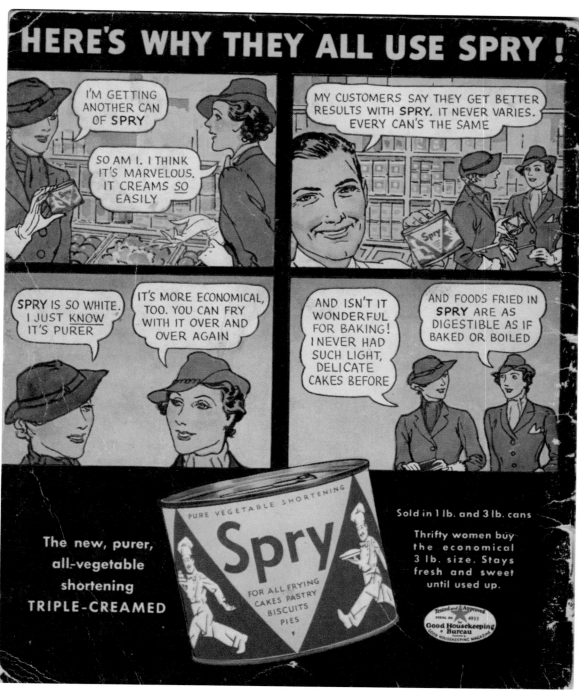

What Shall I Cook Today? / 1936 /
Spry Shortening / Lever Brothers / Back cover

Margarine or oleomargarine was a European invention. German scientists had been experimenting with identifying and separating fatty acids and recombining them into new forms as early as 1813 but what we know as modern margarine is a French product resulting in a call for a cheaper butter alternative from Emperor Napoleon III. (The first Napoleon is the patron of the pressure canner as it was his call to scientists to discover a way to better preserve foods.)

The 1869 patented margarine recipe called for beef tallow and lard to be mixed to varying levels of saturation. Modern margarine recipes vary by manufacturer and can contain a blend of animal and vegetable oils, salt, and milk fat. The food purity law passed in 1905 banned yellow-dyed margarine from being sold as it could be passed off as butter. Like many other ersatz products, World War II lessened legal and consumer resistance and margarine soon found full acceptance. Except in Wisconsin. The Dairy State lobbied Congress to keep margarine white which resulted in a small color packet being sold with the margarine to be mixed in at home. This ban was removed in 1955 while Wisconsin kept its local ban on all margarine sales enacted for a few more years after that.

Sweets with Allsweet Margarine / 1972 / This pamphlet cookbook contracted famed home economist of the era, Martha Logan, to develop recipes and lend her name to their marketing efforts.

Advertisement for Swift's Allsweet Oleomargarine / 1950 / The Swift Company makes a number of appearances throughout modern processed food and food advertising history. It began as a meatpacking house and grew to become one of the infamous Big Five who monopolized the industry through the 1920s. As the company grew, they diversified their holdings through product development and acquisitions. Swift produced many canned meats, shortenings, lards, and margarines. Now owned by Brazilian-based JBS, Swift is part of a conglomerate that makes up the world's largest meatpacking company.

Three Meals A Day—With Nucoa / 1929 / Front and back cover / Nucoa was introduced to consumers in 1917 and grew to become the best-selling margarine in the United States. It merged with Best Foods, makers of Best and Hellman's Mayonnaise.

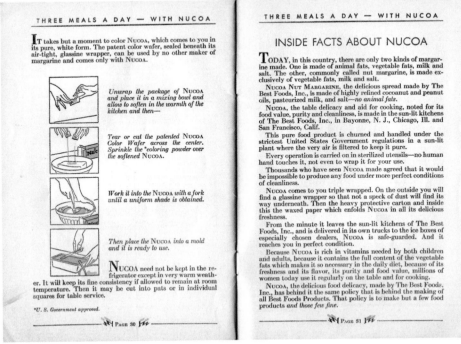

It takes but a moment to color Nucoa, which comes to you in its pure, white form. The patent color wafer, sealed beneath its air-tight, glassine wrapper, can be used by no other maker of margarine and comes only with Nucoa.

Unwrap the package of Nucoa and place it in a mixing bowl and allow to soften in the warmth of the kitchen and then—

Tear or cut the patented Nucoa Color Wafer across the center. Sprinkle the °coloring powder over the softened Nucoa.

Work it into the Nucoa with a fork until a uniform shade is obtained.

Then place the Nucoa into a mold and it is ready to use.

Nucoa need not be kept in the refrigerator except in very warm weather. It will keep its fine consistency if allowed to remain at room temperature. Then it may be cut into pats or in individual squares for table service.

°U. S. Government approved.

INSIDE FACTS ABOUT NUCOA

Today, in this country, there are only two kinds of margarine made. One is made of animal fats, vegetable fats, milk and salt. The other, commonly called nut margarine, is made exclusively of vegetable fats, milk and salt.

Nucoa Nut Margarine, the delicious spread made by The Best Foods, Inc., is made of highly refined cocoanut and peanut oils, pasteurized milk, and salt—*no animal fats*.

Nucoa, the table delicacy and aid for cooking, noted for its food value, purity and cleanliness, is made in the sun-lit kitchens of The Best Foods, Inc., in Bayonne, N. J., Chicago, Ill. and San Francisco, Calif.

This pure food product is churned and handled under the strictest United States Government regulations in a sun-lit plant where the very air is filtered to keep it pure.

Every operation is carried on in sterilized utensils—no human hand touches it, not even to wrap it for your use.

Thousands who have seen Nucoa made agreed that it would be impossible to produce any food under more perfect conditions of cleanliness.

Nucoa comes to you triple wrapped. On the outside you will find a glassine wrapper so that not a speck of dust will find its way underneath. Then the heavy protective carton and inside this the waxed paper which enfolds Nucoa in all its delicious freshness.

From the minute it leaves the sun-lit kitchens of The Best Foods, Inc., and is delivered in its own trucks to the ice boxes of especially chosen dealers, Nucoa is safe-guarded. And it reaches you in perfect condition.

Because Nucoa is rich in vitamins needed by both children and adults, because it contains the full content of the vegetable fats which makes it so necessary in the daily diet, because of its freshness and its flavor, its purity and food value, millions of women today use it regularly on the table and for cooking.

Nucoa, the delicious food delicacy, made by The Best Foods, Inc., has behind it the same policy that is behind the making of all Best Foods Products. That policy is to make but a few food products *and those few fine.*

Three Meals A Day-With Nucoa / 1929 / Inside Facts About Nucoa / Margarine, due to food purity laws, was not allowed to be sold with yellow dye until after World War II. Manufacturers got around the law by including a small dye packet that the user would blend in at home.

37 kitchen-tested recipes for

better eating...easier cooking

the modern way with **PREAM**

Dear Friend:

Every day more and more women are discovering Pream—the delicious new "creamer" for coffee and other beverages. They're discovering, too, what a wonderful *ingredient* Pream is for cooking . . . how convenient to have always on hand because it *keeps* sweet and fresh-tasting without refrigeration.

Here at the Pream Kitchens, we have a continuing program of testing and retesting to develop new recipes that Pream® makes more delicious, easier to prepare and—so often—more economical.

Here, then, is "the cream of the new crop" . . . the top winners in test after test. Try them soon—and often! We hope you like them, and if you'd like copies for friends . . . or if you have some ideas of your own for Pream cookery, do drop us a line.

Cordially,

Sally Ross

Pream Test Kitchens
625 Cleveland Avenue
Columbus 16, Ohio

Better eating...easier cooking / 1958 / Pream / An early entry into the coffee creamer field, Pream was made from dehydrated cream with added sugar. Because of the concentrated milk proteins it did not easily dissolve. Carnation solved this problem in 1958 with the introduction of Coffee-Mate which replaced the milk fats with vegetable oil.

➤ Animal milk is laden with food lore; the high caloric content makes it a desirable human food but pathogens find high-fat, low-acid dairy to be a perfect disease vector. Food preservation technology from the turn of the 19th century that removed moisture by dehydration and combined with canning extended the usability of milk. Powdered milk was a safe and cheaper alternative to keeping a cow. Canned or evaporated milk, with 40% of the water removed, is shelf-stable for up to two years. With the now abundance of milk, companies of course thought of new ways to use the milk products.

IN YOUR

SPARKLE MEALS

RECIPES BY
MARY LEE TAYLOR

★STARRING—
Light-Luscious
Low-calorie
Whipped Topping
and Desserts
Page 4-5

Sparkle In Your Meals / 1958 / PET Instant
Nonfat Dry Milk / Front and back cover

INSTANTLY YOURS

One of the charms of this wild profession of homemaking is the unexpectedness of it all. A solitary noon snack blossoms into a neighborly luncheon for four. Dinnertime arrives at the end of a busy day and there's no dessert waiting to greet the hungry troops.

All good reasons to be protected with Dessert Insurance, several packages of instant pudding and trimmings on hand in the cupboard shelf. You can make up a variety of smooth, creamy desserts *without cooking*, in less time than it would take you to rush down to the store for a ready-made dessert.

Reach into the refrigerator, the candy jar, the jelly shelf for additions to your pudding treats. If you've mixed up a 4-serving package of pudding, for instance, you might try stirring in any of these for flavor:

> ½ to ¾ cup diced bananas, peaches, apricots
> ½ to ¾ cup fresh strawberries, blueberries, grapes
> 2 to 4 tablespoons chopped nuts, crushed peppermint candy,
>   grated chocolate
> ¼ to ½ cup mixed candied fruits

With plain pudding, pass around a small tray of toppings, or add these touches to each serving: a spoonful of chilled canned cranberry jelly, a drizzle of chocolate syrup, a tablespoon of honey, a covering of just-thawed frozen fruit—strawberries, raspberries, or mixed fruit.

With the basic mix so quick to prepare, you'll have time to try some interesting variations. Applesauce, with a dash of nutmeg and cinnamon, enlivens a Spiced Apple Pudding. Sour cream blends into a Piquant Pudding. And here's the final surprise: instant pudding whips into a Coffee Float, a frothy dessert-drink that could be the hit of any impromptu party.

3

'Dessert Insurance' / Instantly Yours / 1965 / General Foods /
A collection of recipes featuring all of General Foods' instant products
including Dream Whip, Minute Tapioca, and Jell-O®.

TV's zaniest couple...
BURNS and
ALLEN
Every week—CBS-TV Network

©Walt Disney Productions

Nation's top children show...
MICKEY MOUSE CLUB
ABC-TV Network
5:00 to 6:00 P.M. Week Days

New kind of cookbook...
The COOK'S HANDBOOK

96 pages of how-to-do-it ideas and illustrations. Full-color food photographs and selected recipes.

Send 35¢ in coin for your copy to:
Home Service Department FF-7—**Carnation Company**, Los Angeles **19**, California

EVAPORATED MILK

the better-blending milk for all your cook

108

Carnation's Family Favorites / 1956 / Carnation Company / Front and back cover /
The recipes were developed by popular home economist Mary Blake who was the
director of Carnation's Home Service Department. The back cover informs consumers of two television programs sponsored by the company. Unlike today where
advertisements are purchased by block of time and program, corporations provided the financial support for an entire program. Stars and featured actors would
present endorsements of the products between acts and during scene breaks.

Sauces

NO OTHER FORM OF MILK HAS SO MANY USES

- Carnation's special-blending qualities give a smoothness to your sauces and gravies not possible with any other form of milk.

- In the Carnation "Lump-Free" Cream Sauce recipe below, you need only half as much flour and shortening — and in the easy, inexpensive Cheese Sauce recipe, no flour or shortening is needed! Carnation's special-blending qualities make it possible.

- Use these basic recipes for your favorite casseroles — or serve over well-drained vegetables. You'll discover how much smoother — and how much easier — your sauces can be when made with Carnation.

LUMP-FREE CREAM SAUCE

(Makes about 1 cup)

    1 tablespoon butter
    1 tablespoon flour
    ½ teaspoon salt
    1 cup undiluted Carnation
        Evaporated Milk

Melt butter in top of double boiler. Add flour and salt. Stir until smooth. Slowly add Carnation. Place over boiling water. Cook until thickened and smooth (about 10 minutes), stirring constantly.

CHEESE SAUCE

(Makes about 2½ cups)

    1-2/3 cups (large can) undiluted
        Carnation Evaporated Milk
    ½ teaspoon salt
    2 cups (about 8 ounces) grated
        process-type American cheese

Simmer Carnation and salt in saucepan over low heat to just below boiling point (about 2 to 3 minutes). Add cheese and stir until thickened and smooth (about 1 to 2 minutes longer).

8

110

The famous share their famous Carnation Evaporated Milk recipes

Next time you yearn for a real chocolate sundae, try Rosey's fast fudge sauce. Just plain milk doesn't make it. You'll need Carnation Evaporated Milk for that rich, thick texture.

FUDGE SAUCE A LA ROSEY

| 1 large can undiluted Velvetized Carnation Evaporated Milk | 3 squares unsweetened chocolate |
| 2 cups sugar | 1 teaspoon vanilla |

Mix Carnation, sugar and chocolate in saucepan. Bring to boil over medium heat. Cook 5 minutes, stirring vigorously. Remove from heat. Add vanilla. Beat with rotary beater for 1 minute. Serve hot or chilled on ice cream or cake. If the sauce seems a bit too thick, just add **undiluted** Carnation and blend before serving. (Makes 2½ cups sauce.)

Carnation® Evaporated Milk, Carnation Company, Los Angeles, California

Carnation's Family Favorites / 1956 / Lump-Free Cream Sauce & Cheese Sauce / Carnation Company

The famous share their famous Carnation Evaporated Milk recipes / 1970 / Carnation Company / Magazine advertisement / Featuring popular football player and actor Rosey Grier, this ad includes a recipe for fudge sauce.

➤ Dehydration and packaging technology drove food manufacturers to introduce new products to the food landscape. Removing moisture and oxygen from foods prevents decay and germs so foods could be cooked then dehydrated and sold to consumers. Just add water, and you would have a wide array of quick and easy foods. Instant coffee, instant tea, instant potatoes, instant everything!

Easy Triumphs with the New Minute Tapioca / 1934 / General Foods / Front and back cover / Invented in 1880s by Mary Travers, the 'minute' of Minute Tapioca was her idea to grind the manioc (or cassava) root through a coffee grinder to render the cooked product smoother. She sold her patent in 1894 to grocer and publisher John Whitman who named it Minute Tapioca and began publishing cookbooks with hundreds of recipes using tapioca in every way imaginable. He sold the company in 1926 to the Postum Company who recently acquired the Jell-O® brand. Postum renamed itself General Foods a few years later and continued to innovate food processing including the invention of Minute Rice in 1949.

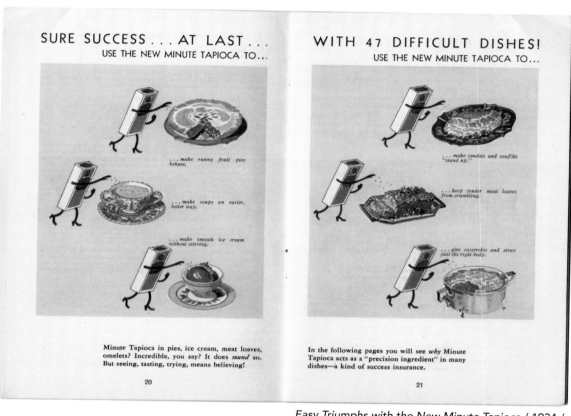

SURE SUCCESS...AT LAST...
USE THE NEW MINUTE TAPIOCA TO...

...make runny fruit pies behave.

...make soups an easier, better way.

...make smooth ice cream without stirring.

Minute Tapioca in pies, ice cream, meat loaves, omelets? Incredible, you say? It does *sound* so. But seeing, tasting, trying, means believing!

20

WITH 47 DIFFICULT DISHES!
USE THE NEW MINUTE TAPIOCA TO...

...make omelets and soufflés "stand up."

...keep tender meat loaves from crumbling.

...give casseroles and stews just the right body.

In the following pages you will see *why* Minute Tapioca acts as a "precision ingredient" in many dishes—a kind of success insurance.

21

Easy Triumphs with the New Minute Tapioca / 1934 / Use the new Minute Tapioca to... / General Foods / Centerfold pages

Mystery Meats

➤ Upton Sinclair changed how Americans consume meat
with his 1906 novel *The Jungle*. In it, he explored the lives of
immigrant workers at meatpacking plants in Chicago and
the conditions of where they worked, and of the utter filth in
which livestock were slaughtered. Food scams and scares
were commonplace throughout American history, but it took
Sinclair's book to generate the required outrage needed for
the federal government to take action. It was the beginning
of the Meat Inspection Act and later the Pure Food and Drug
Act. As Sinclair famously said, "I aimed at the public's heart,
and by accident I hit it in the stomach."

*The Great Taste of Spam® / 1994 / Snacks and
Appetizers, Spicy SPAM® Party Dip, SPAM® Quesadillas,
and SPAM® Cantina Appetizers / Hormel Foods*

SPAM® 'N' Limas / 1946 /
Hormel Foods /
Magazine advertisement

SPAM® 'N' Macaroni Loaf / 1946 /
Hormel Foods /
Magazine advertisement

There's Ham in SPAM® / 1946 /
Hormel Foods /
Magazine advertisement

Sausages and Luncheon Meats

These meats may be made from all pork, all beef or a combination of two or more meats. Most wieners (also referred to as frankfurters) are precooked and can be eaten without cooking although they are usually heated to enhance the flavor. The canned luncheon meat can be served either cold or heated.

Try this idea for dressing up canned luncheon meat — Orange-Glazed Luncheon Meat, page 76.

Pillsbury Meat Cookbook / Orange Glazed SPAM® / 1969 /
Pillsbury Company / This recipe notes that 'luncheon meat' was
the main ingredient; the choice of SPAM® or Treet is yours.

➤ Canned and potted meats have been a part of American cuisine since the founding, but these were dishes that were either preserved at home or a trusted local butcher. The newly enacted laws enabled larger meat packers to thrive as they quickly adopted new sanitary technologies and new mechanized canning tools. World War I put the new technologies to the test as the challenge to feed armies and navies motivated companies to find new ways to deliver high-quality proteins. During the war years, all sorts of canned meats were sent to soldiers and sailors, from pork and beans to coq au vin. After the war, demobilized troops, accustomed to the canned meats, looked for the products at home. Companies worked to improve the taste and quality for the civilian market and the first large-scale commercially canned meat products arrived on grocery shelves in the early 1920s. The Oscar Mayer Company was developing its plastic sealing systems on bacon and soft sausages while the Hormel Company introduced SPAM® to the world in 1937.

Marie Gifford's 168 Meal Planning Ideas that start with Armour Star Canned Meats /
1959 / Armour and Company / Front and back cover

Treet / 1959 / *Marie Gifford's 168 Meal Planning Ideas* / Armour and Company /
Treet was Armour and Company's answer to Hormel's popular SPAM® product.

➤ Consumers one hundred years ago were less squeamish about meat than we are today. Wealth, culture, and availability all played a role in shaping our collective appetites. Meat was expensive and not something served every single day at every single meal—nothing was wasted. Potted meat, the forefather of modern canned meats, was an old preservation method of using fats to seal spiced ground meats against airborne contamination. Twentieth-century meat packers took inspiration and created a wide range of canned meat products. They've gained a dubious reputation of late. High in fat and salt (both preservatives), they are made from the by-products of the butchering process, once described by the chief meat inspector at the Patrick Cudahy Meat Packing plant as being made of "inways, outways, and throughways."

A Vitality Meat So Good To Eat / c. 1930s / Wilson & Company, Inc. / Magazine advertisement / The Wilson Meat Packing Company was based in Kansas City and considered one of the Big Four meat packers in the United States (Wilson, Cudahy, Armour, and Swift.) It closed operations and ceased production of its brands in early 1976. MOR was their version of Hormel's SPAM®.

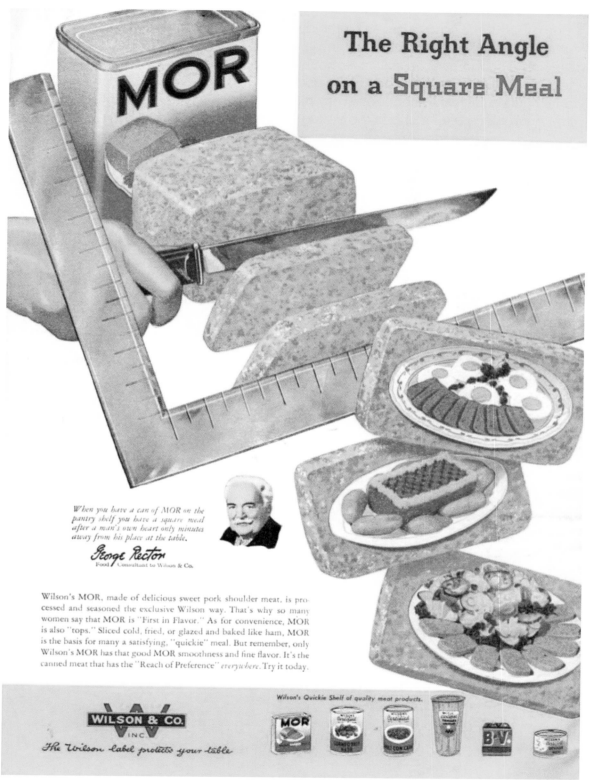

The Right Angle on a Square Meal

When you have a can of MOR on the pantry shelf you have a square meal after a man's own heart only minutes away from his place at the table.

George Rector
Food Consultant to Wilson & Co.

Wilson's MOR, made of delicious sweet pork shoulder meat, is processed and seasoned the exclusive Wilson way. That's why so many women say that MOR is "First in Flavor." As for convenience, MOR is also "tops." Sliced cold, fried, or glazed and baked like ham, MOR is the basis for many a satisfying, "quickie" meal. But remember, only Wilson's MOR has that good MOR smoothness and fine flavor. It's the canned meat that has the "Reach of Preference" *everywhere.* Try it today.

WILSON & CO. INC
The Wilson label protects your table

Wilson's Quickie Shelf of quality meat products.

The Right Angle on a Square Meal / c. 1947 / Wilson & Company, Inc. / Magazine advertisement

➤ The advertising golden age of the 1950s and 60s saw the large meatpacking companies competing to gain a foothold in middle-class American kitchens. Canned meats were marketed as a readily prepared equal substitute to other meat proteins. The home economists on staff at Armour, Hormel, Wilson, and others worked to develop and adapt recipes that could use canned meats. Some of these dishes were more successful than others. For every hipster SPAM® onigiri, there's a SPAM® and lima bean casserole lurking in the dark corners of someone's childhood.

CHICKEN DISH IDEAS
by
SWANSON
and Super-Strength
ALCOA WRAP

WE USED IT AND WE LIKE IT
USE-TESTED
BY
McCall's

CHICKEN DISH
IDEAS
by
SWANSON
and Super-Strength
ALCOA WRAP

WE USED IT AND WE LIKE IT
USE-TESTED
BY
McCall's

*Chicken Dish Ideas by Swanson and Alcoa Wrap / 1960 /
Alcoa Aluminum Company & Swanson / Front and back cover*

Chicken Fricassee with Vegetables

1 can Swanson Chicken
in Golden Gravy
½ cup cooked and drained peas,
lima beans, or mixed vegetables
1 tablespoon chopped pimiento

In saucepan, combine all ingredients. Heat slowly until thoroughly hot. Serve over toast or split biscuits. 2 generous servings.

TIP: To make quick biscuits, arrange packaged refrigerator biscuits, or biscuits made from mix, on double thick sheet of Alcoa Wrap so that they just touch each other. Place on oven rack. Bake according to package directions. Pull rack out; fold foil lightly around biscuits to keep them warm.

Chicketti

(pictured above)

1 can Swanson Boned
Chicken or Turkey
1 can (15¼ ounces)
Franco-American Spaghetti
2 tablespoons minced parsley
Dash garlic salt
½ cup shredded mild
process cheese

Combine boned chicken, spaghetti, parsley, and garlic salt; spoon into shallow baking pan or 1-quart casserole which has been lined with Alcoa Wrap. Sprinkle cheese on top. Bake in a moderate oven (350°F.) about 20 minutes. 2 to 3 servings.

A la King 'n Noodles au Gratin

1 can Swanson Chicken a la King
⅓ cup shredded mild process cheese
1 tablespoon chopped parsley
2 cups cooked noodles
(about 4 ounces uncooked)

In saucepan, combine chicken a la king, cheese, and parsley. Heat until cheese is melted; stir now and then. Fold in cooked noodles; heat a few minutes longer. Serve in individual casseroles made from Alcoa Wrap. 3 servings.

TIP: Make individual casseroles by shaping a double thickness of Alcoa Wrap over a cup or small bowl; turn edges under and crimp.

Chicken Noodle Bake

1 can Campbell's Cream
of Celery Soup
½ cup milk
1 can Swanson Boned
Chicken or Turkey
2 cups cooked noodles
(about 4 ounces uncooked)
1 cup cooked lima beans
2 tablespoons diced pimiento
¼ cup buttered bread crumbs

Blend soup and milk; add chicken, cooked noodles, lima beans, and pimiento. Spoon into 1½-quart casserole which has been lined with Alcoa Wrap; sprinkle crumbs on top. Bake in a moderate oven (375°F.) about 25 minutes. 4 servings.

Creamed Chicken with Mushrooms

1 can (3 ounces) sliced
mushrooms, drained
1 tablespoon minced onion
2 teaspoons butter or margarine
1 can Campbell's Cream
of Chicken Soup
¼ cup milk
1 can Swanson Boned
Chicken or Turkey
1 tablespoon minced parsley
1½ cups cooked noodles
(about 3 ounces uncooked)
Slivered toasted almonds

In saucepan, cook mushrooms and onion in butter; blend in soup, milk, chicken, and parsley. Heat; stir often. Serve over hot noodles; garnish with almonds. 2 to 3 servings.

TIP: If desired, serve creamed chicken over split baked potatoes instead of noodles . . . wrap potatoes in Alcoa Wrap before baking.

SWANSON IS A TRADEMARK OF *Campbell* SOUP COMPANY

Super-Strength Alcoa Wrap is available in both regular and heavy duty weights with a complete line of sizes.

PRINTED IN U. S. A., 1960   No. 80779

Chicken Fricassee, Chicketti, A la King 'n Noodles au Gratin, Chicken Noodle Bake, and Creamed Chicken with Mushrooms / 1960 / *Chicken Dish Ideas by Swanson and Alcoa Wrap* / Alcoa Aluminum Company & Swanson

Gingered Pear and Chicken Salad

1 package lime flavored gelatin
1 cup hot water
1 cup ginger ale
3 tablespoons lime juice
8 pear halves
1 envelope unflavored gelatin
½ cup cold water
1 egg yolk
1 can cream of celery soup
1 egg white, beaten stiff
1 6-ounce can SWANSON BONED CHICKEN, cubed
½ cup whipping cream, whipped

"After saving your Swanson recipes because they are so attractive as well as delicious, I have decided to send you this boned chicken recipe that has been in our family for several years."

Mrs. Leavenworth Wheeler, Yuma, Arizona

Dissolve lime flavored gelatin in hot water. Cool until mixture starts to thicken. Add ginger ale; spoon over pear halves arranged in 1½ quart ring mold. Chill.

Dissolve gelatin in cold water. Add egg yolk to soup and heat to boiling. Remove from heat and stir in gelatin. Chill until mixture thickens slightly. Lightly fold in remaining ingredients. Pour carefully over jelled lime layer. Chill until firm—about 4 hours. Unmold on bed of lettuce or chicory. Serves 8.

Perfect for a buffet luncheon or dinner.

Serve with Potato Ruffles or Shoe String Potatoes and hot rolls. Rich devil's food cake and coffee will complete a nutritious and hearty meal.

9

Sue Swanson's Chicken and Turkey Recipes from 24 Good Cooks /
Gingered Pear and Chicken Salad / 1954 / Swanson Company

"I've found Swanson Boned Turkey a wonderful time-saver, and combining it with cranberry sauce this way gives it such a partified air. It can be used for Sunday night supper or a bridge party with excellent results."

Mrs. August W. Beikirch, Rochester, New York

Cranberry Mousse

1 tablespoon unflavored gelatin
¼ cup cold water
1 can whole cranberry sauce
1 teaspoon grated orange rind
1 teaspoon grated lemon rind
2 tablespoons orange juice
1 can SWANSON BONED TURKEY, diced
½ cup whipping cream, whipped

Place gelatin in custard cup. Add cold water and let stand 2 minutes. Place custard cup in pan of boiling water until gelatin dissolves.

Crush cranberry sauce with a fork; stir in gelatin. Add orange and lemon rind and the orange juice, mix. Chill until mixture begins to set. Fold in Boned Turkey and whipped cream.

Pour into 6 individual molds (½ cup for each) and chill 1 to 2 hours or until firm.

Unmold on lettuce cups and garnish with watercress or parsley. Serve with fluffy mayonnaise dressing.

7

Sue Swanson's Chicken and Turkey Recipes from 24 Good Cooks /
Cranberry Mousse / 1954 / Swanson Company

Underwood Jumbo...heap zesty Underwood Deviled Ham on split French roll. Top with onion and green pepper rings. Makes a man-size sandwich that's packed with flavor, packed with nutrition – thanks to Underwood's whole-ham goodness!

Picnic Pack...New! Add cheese to a tangy Underwood Deviled Ham sandwich. Wrap in aluminum foil and toast on your outdoor grill, in your oven... or eat as is. Tastes wonderful, grilled or not!

Deviled Pineapple Sandwich...cover slices of bread with plenty of smooth-spreading Underwood Deviled Ham. Top with juicy pineapple slice and broil. Underwood's adds real, fine-ham flavor...costs just pennies!

UNDERWOOD DEVILED HAM

glorifies "take along" or "eat at home" sandwiches!

Underwood Deviled Ham adds tempting flavor...hearty eating enjoyment! It's a "must" for summer sandwiches, salads and snacks . . . wonderful for main dishes, too! That's why it's by far the leading brand, *best* for spreads, *best* for cooking. Buy Underwood Deviled Ham in the Family Size can *and* the Regular Size.

Wm. Underwood Co., Watertown 72, Mass.

22

Glorifies everyday foods

UNDER WOOD Family Size DEVILED HAM

WOOD DEVILED HAM

Underwood Deviled Ham / c. 1950s / William Underwood Company / Magazine advertisement

➤ The heyday of canned meats from the 1920s to the 1970s gave way to a more health-conscious American society that had access to cheaper whole-muscle proteins. Many brands are discontinued while some remain regionally popular. Only the Hormel Company's SPAM® maintains steady sales in the 21st century, and that's due to the worldwide exposure the brand enjoyed during World War II when it was shipped to every corner of the Earth to feed both soldiers and civilians. Many Pacific Island recipes have incorporated SPAM® into their regional dishes to the extent that SPAM® is now an identifying ingredient of Hawaiian cuisine.

What's for Dinner? / c. 1930s / Fort Pitt Meats - Fried & Reineman Packing Company / Front cover

What's for Dinner? / Tempting Cold Cuts for
Tasty Bites / c. 1930s / Fort Pitt Meats -
Fried & Reineman Packing Company

A Good Housewife

➤ Since the early 1920s when Edward Bernays convinced women that smoking would keep them thin, marketers have sent subtle, and not so subtle, messages equating foods with weight loss. Before there was a diet-food industry that used chemical substitutes for fats and sugars, advertisers made dubious claims about the caloric content of their foods. (For the record, 1 cup of Campbell's tomato soup made with water is 180 calories but is 283 calories when made with whole milk.)

The Story Cottage Cheese tells in your mirror / 1930 / The Dairy and Food Bureau of Chicago / Front cover

'Surprise! Soup Shakes!' / 1956 / Campbell's Soup Company / Magazine advertisement / This ad was part a short-lived campaign to encourage women of to drink a 'soup shake' as a meal.

Help Yourself To A Prettier Figure / 1963 /
Heinz Corporation / Front cover

Summer Salad Bowl / 1963 / *Help Yourself To A
Prettier Figure* / Heinz Corporation

➤ If you think the outrageous 'one-upmanship' of children's birthday parties is a recent phenomenon, you'd be wrong. Women have always been judged by how they raise their children, and as the notion of what childhood was changed in the post-Victorian era, the race to outdo the neighbors was on. It was a mark of wealth and class that your children weren't working in a factory and to be entertained in the same (albeit kid-ified) high style. The most American of values, faking it until you make it, was an important element of belonging and women were encouraged to adopt the habits of the so-called 'upper classes.'

What's all this about Mother not wanting to make so many cakes? / 1920 / Baker's Coconut / Franklin Baker Coconut Company / Unfolded pamphlet / Baker's Coconut became part of General Foods in 1927.

KEEP THEIR DAYS CRAMMED WITH *Surprises*

THEY'RE young for so short a period—it's hard to keep from wanting to give them surprises and parties, all the time. Since little folks like to have a hand in preparing for their gay occasions, we've worked out a simple cookie recipe they can make.

CHILDREN'S PARTY REFRESHMENTS	FLOWER COOKIES *(Illustrated above)*	
Strawberry and Chocolate Ice Cream in Shells	½ cup butter	2¼ teaspoons baking powder
°Flower Cookies	1 cup sugar	¼ teaspoon salt
Milk	1 egg	1 tablespoon milk
	1½ cups flour	¾ teaspoon vanilla

Thirty

1. Cream the butter, add the sugar gradually and cream thoroughly.
2. Add the egg and beat well.
3. Mix and sift the flour, baking powder and salt and add to the first mixture alternately with the milk.
4. Add the vanilla and chill for ½ hour.
5. Roll out on a floured board to about ⅛ inch thickness.
6. Cut in the shape of tulips, daisies or other flowers with a floured cooky cutter.
7. Place on an unbuttered cooky sheet.
8. Bake in a moderately hot oven (375° F.) for 8 to 10 minutes.

Make **Frosting** as follows:

1½ cups sifted confectioners sugar	2 tablespoons milk
Few grains salt	Yellow, red or green coloring
¼ teaspoon vanilla	Cocoa

1. Mix the sugar, salt and vanilla
2. Add enough milk to make the mixture soft enough to spread.
3. Add yellow, red or green coloring as desired and spread on cookies.
4. To make brown centers for daisies add a little cocoa to the plain frosting. This recipe makes about 32 flower cookies.

Thirty-one

Sealtest Food Advisor / 1941 / Keep Their Days Crammed With Surprises / Sealtest Dairy

"My First Day in the Kitchen"

My first day in the kitchen, I *watched!* Mother knows all about cooking, but I had to learn about knives, bowls, and kitchen things. (Mom calls them "utensils".)

MIXING BOWLS are used a lot in our kitchen. Some of them are plastic, some are china. Mother calls the glass ones "heat proof" because they can be put in the oven. Usually mixing bowls come in sets like these:

Small — for beating eggs whipping cream sandwich filling storing food in refrigerator

Medium — for salads puddings pie crust muffins

Large — for cake batter cookies pie fillings

There are *two kinds of MEASURING CUPS* in our kitchen. For sugar and flour we use

¼ cup ⅓ cup ½ cup 1 cup

I learned to spoon sugar into the cup and level off the sugar like this

For *milk* or *water*, I use glass cups with a big handle and a pouring lip. I gave Mother a set for Christmas that looked like this:

1 cup 2 cup (1 pint) 4 cup (1 quart)

4

SAUCEPANS are made of metal (like aluminum) or heat-proof glass. Some are pretty ones with copper bottoms. Use saucepans

Covered for cooking vegetables (like potatoes) preparing stews cooking rice cooking cereals

Uncovered for sauces puddings cocoa soup

KNIVES Our knives are kept in a drawer that has a wooden holder. (That way the knife blades don't get dull...I don't get my fingers cut, either.)

Paring Knife — I use this for cleaning vegetables.

Cutting Knife — Mother uses this for dicing carrots, slicing celery.

Carving Knife — Dad uses this for carving roast beef, slicing turkey.

P.S. You won't get cut if you handle a paring knife carefully. Cut away from your hands. And use a wooden board for slicing vegetables like carrots!

MEASURING SPOONS come in sets like these. Mine are colored plastic...with a different color for the ¼, ½, 1 teaspoon and 1 tablespoon. Some measuring spoons are aluminum. When I use measuring spoons for dry ingredients, I always level the spoon off with a spatula.

RUBBER SCRAPER...gets *every* bit of pudding, cake batter or icing out of the bowl. (And it is easier to clean the bowl afterwards.)

WOODEN SPOONS...are for mixing salads, instant puddings or sauces. When I cook, I use a wooden spoon for stirring. Wooden spoons have extra-long handles that make it easier to mix...and the handle never gets hot or burns my hand!

VEGETABLE PEELER. I use this for cleaning carrots, peeling potatoes or apples and cleaning celery. A vegetable peeler is so easy to use...and fast!

EGG BEATER. Used for beating eggs or whipping Carnation Evaporated Milk. (You'll find out how easy it is to whip Carnation on page 33.)

5

Fun to Cookbook / 1971 / "My First Day in the Kitchen" / Carnation Company / The Carnation Company created this cookbook aimed at young girls to take part in the growing trend of marketing directly to children. It also served to reinforce traditional, Puritan-influenced gender roles.

➤ Advertisers struggled with the growing women's empowerment movements. Many chose to focus on 'entertaining' as the peg on which to hang their marketing. From creating buffet meals for a crowd to outdoor barbeque picnics to young single working women, everyone loves a party. Through it all, the messages of the 'correct' way to be a woman are loud and clear.

A handbook on party-giving for the young hostess
A reference guide for class and club entertainment committees

You're Entertaining / 1961 / Scott Paper Company / Front cover

How to Plan a Successful Menu

VEGETABLES AND FRUITS

4 or more servings
Include dark green or yellow
vegetables; citrus fruit or tomatoes

Festive Foods / 1969 / How to Plan a
Successful Menu / Wisconsin Gas Company

CAN'T YOU JUST
SEE YOURSELF?

PRAISED... ADMIRED

134

ENVIED... APPRECIATED!

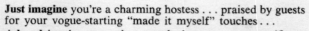

Just imagine you're a charming hostess . . . praised by guests for your vogue-starting "made it myself" touches . . .

Adored by the man who secretly knows your magnificent barbecue sauce adds the master touch to his outdoor cooking . . .

Envied by "The Girls" for that *exclusive* orange souffle (made with your very own marmalade!) served at your bridge luncheon . . .

Famous for your corn relish that always goes over big at bazaars . . .

Loved for traditional goodies your children will fondly remember and talk of you making as long as they live!

Like what you see? Good! Read on . . .

Can't You Just See Yourself? / 1966 / Praised...Admired...Envied...Appreciated! / Ball Brothers Company / Ball canning jars took a novel approach to marketing home food preservation to young women in 1966, appealing to a need for outside social validation.

➤ The birth of the modern age in the 20th Century was to the whirring buzz and rattle of machines. "Home Service" electricity went from 100k rural homes in 1920 to 4.5 million in 1956. Having electricity was a national priority and a necessity to becoming a part of the middle class. Radio and television programs directed at women and sponsored by manufacturers used actresses to extol the virtues of the blender, oven, or mixer being sold.

In the 1950s and '60s, gas and electric companies across the country employed home economists to develop recipes that required either gas- or electric-powered tools. These cookbooks taught consumers how to cook with the newfangled electric and gas stoves and encouraged them to buy more gadgets (which of course meant buying more electricity).

The introduction of microwave ovens began a new cycle of cookbooks from manufacturers, food processors, and councils offering a plethora of ways to use their products in microwave cooking.

GAS BRINGS YOU
ALL THE COMFORTS OF HOME
instantly, automatically, economically

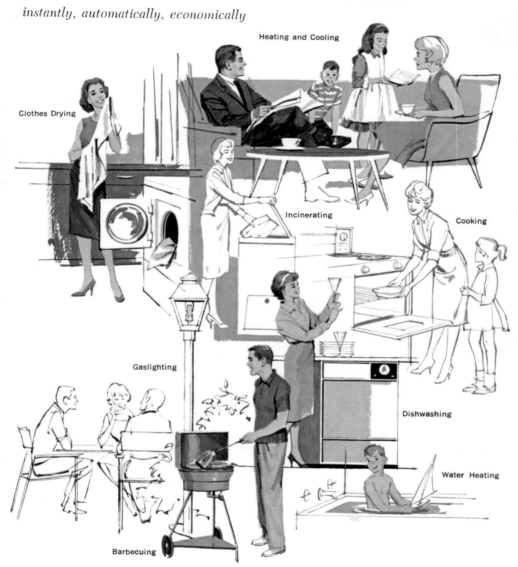

Gas Brings You All The Comforts Of Home / 1962 /
Wisconsin Gas Company Festive Foods / Back cover

MICROWAVE MAGIC

Recipes
From
Your
Oklahoma Peanut Commission

Microwave Magic / 1984 /
Oklahoma Peanut Commission /
Front and back cover / Microwave ovens were
introduced to consumers in the late 1970s and took
another decade before they became a kitchen staple.

Corning's Microwave Browners / c. 1970s / Corning Glass Works / Front cover /
Microwave ovens in American homes are primarily used as a warming and defrosting
device, but early advocates promoted them as the end-all, be-all of easy cooking.
A noticeable side effect of microwave cooking is the absence of the Maillard Effect,
the browning of meats through heat, which left meats cooked in a microwave pale,
grey and unappetizing. The Corning Glass Company saw the opportunity to relaunch
their glass cookware as 'browners' for microwave cooking.

The Mystery Ingredient

➤ Joint marketing. Cross-promotion. Whatever you called it, corporate food producers expanded their offerings in the 20th century to become diversified holding companies that sold every-thing from soap to shortening to snacks.

'A Delicious Salad for Dinner Tonight' / c. 1930s / General Foods / A multiple-brand grocery store display advertisement that is the harbinger of a future where incongruent ingredients were mixed together and sacrificed to the gods of marketing.

Downright Delicious Sun-Maid Raisin Recipes / 1950 / H.J. Heinz Company / Front and back cover / The covers show dishes that are familiar, oatmeals, muffins, and bread, but lurking amidst the sweets are recipes for raisin-laden meatloaf and spare ribs.

Quick & Easy
CASSEROLES

OVER 100 SUPERB RECIPES! MOST ARE READY TO BAKE IN 15 MINUTES OR LESS!

Quick & Easy Casseroles / 1988 /
McCormick & Company / Front cover

➤ Invented in 1955, the loved and loathed French's / Durkee's Green Bean Casserole is still served as part of many a holiday feast. French's, inventor of creamy yellow mustard, took on the fried onion product as part of a series of acquisitions and partnerships. Dorcas Reilly, a product of Drexel University's Home Economics program, worked for Campbell's Soup where, in a fit of inspiration, she found the right combination of umami that appealed to the American palate—a salty, creamy, crunchy, fatty mix of one can each of mushroom soup, green beans, and fried onions.

ORIGINAL GREEN BEAN CASSEROLE ►

Ready to bake in just 5 easy minutes

2 cans (16 ounces *each*) cut
green beans, drained or
2 packages (9 ounces *each*)
frozen cut green beans,
cooked and drained
¾ cup milk

1 can (10¾ ounces) condensed
cream of mushroom soup
⅛ teaspoon Durkee Ground
Black Pepper
1 can (2.8 ounces) Durkee
French Fried Onions

Preheat oven to 350°. In medium bowl, combine beans, milk, soup, pepper and ½ can French Fried Onions; pour into 1½-quart casserole. Bake, uncovered, at 350° for 30 minutes or until heated through. Top with remaining onions; bake, uncovered, 5 minutes or until onions are golden brown. *Makes 6 servings*

MICROWAVE DIRECTIONS: Prepare green bean mixture as above; pour into 1½-quart microwave-safe casserole. Cook, covered, on HIGH 8 to 10 minutes or until heated through. Stir beans halfway through cooking time. Top with remaining onions; cook, uncovered, 1 minute. Let stand 5 minutes.

SWISS VEGETABLE MEDLEY ►

Ready to bake in just 5 easy minutes

1 bag (16 ounces) frozen
vegetable combination
(broccoli, carrots,
cauliflower), thawed and
drained
1 can (10¾ ounces) condensed
cream of mushroom soup
1 cup (4 ounces) shredded
Swiss cheese

⅓ cup sour cream
¼ teaspoon Durkee Ground
Black Pepper
1 jar (4 ounces) diced
pimiento, drained
(optional)
1 can (2.8 ounces) Durkee
French Fried Onions

Preheat oven to 350°. In large bowl, combine vegetables, soup, ½ cup cheese, the sour cream, pepper, pimiento and ½ can French Fried Onions. Pour into shallow 1-quart casserole. Bake, covered, at 350° for 30 minutes or until vegetables are done. Sprinkle remaining cheese and onions in diagonal rows across top; bake, uncovered, 5 minutes or until onions are golden brown. *Makes 6 servings*

MICROWAVE DIRECTIONS: Prepare vegetable mixture as above; pour into shallow 1-quart microwave-safe casserole. Cook, covered, on HIGH 8 to 10 minutes or until vegetables are done. Stir vegetables halfway through cooking time. Top with remaining cheese and onions as above; cook, uncovered, 1 minute or until cheese melts. Let stand 5 minutes.

84   EXPRESS VEGGIES, PASTA & MORE

Original Green Bean Casserole and Swiss Vegetable Medley / 1988 / *Quick & Easy Casseroles* / McCormick & Company

Mayonnaise is a tricky bit of French-style cooking to master. It requires a delicate hand to keep the consistency without the separate elements 'breaking' and the sauce falling into a gloppy mess. The advent of a safe, processed version was a time-saving boon for harried cooks.

The first jarred mayo was launched in 1907 in Philadelphia by Amelia Schlorer, but it is the Hellmann's brand founded at the same time in New York City that is still sold today. Hellman's brand is sold on the East Coast while the same product is sold as Best on the West Coast. Mayonnaise was featured in all American cookbooks, and its making taught in the cooking schools. The commercial version quickly replaced the homemade version, and because it was a pantry staple, marketers charged their respective home economics departments to devise as many recipes as possible using the stuff.

IF YOU WANT TO BE HAPPY WHEN COMPANY COMES...

Build an easy, low-point-cost menu around this Super Supper Salad Loaf!

DON'T FOOL YOURSELF...

Real Mayonnaise makes a real difference

The real thing! *Real* Mayonnaise is made with eggs freshly broken from the shell, extra egg yolks, "Fresh-Press" salad oil, vinegar, seasonings. Nothing else! It is all luscious *real mayonnaise*.

Really fresh! Mayonnaise tastes as fresh as the oil that's in it. The fine salad oil in *Real* Mayonnaise is our own "Fresh-Press"—prepared fresh each day, as needed.

Real economy! Because it's all rich, *Real* Mayonnaise, you can stretch it with milk or fruit juice and it's *still* creamy-rich. Doesn't turn watery ... stays on the food you eat instead of running off onto the plate you wash!

Real nutrition! This *Real* Mayonnaise is rich in food energy ... provides almost exactly the same amount, spoonful for spoonful, as vitaminized margarine, or butter. Good for many of the same uses, too—to help you keep wartime rationed menus up to your own proud "taste good" standard.

GROW MORE IN '44

SUPPER FOR SIX

Cream of Tomato Soup
Celery   Crackers
SUPER SALAD LOAF
Corn Sticks   Nucoa
Fresh Pineapple Mint Cup
Ginger Cookies   Coffee

Recipe: **Super Salad Loaf**

Scoop out center of a 1½ pound piece of bologna, leaving a shell.* Soak 1 tbsp. plain gelatin in 2 tbsp. cold water and dissolve over hot water. Mix 1¼ cups cooked mashed peas with 1 tbsp. *Real* Mayonnaise, 2 tsp. minced onion, ½ tsp. salt, ¼ tsp. pepper. Add dissolved gelatin and pack into bologna shell. Chill thoroughly. Place on platter on salad greens. Heap with *Real* Mayonnaise. Garnish with radish roses, parsley and onion rings, as illustrated.

*NOTE: Use left-over bologna in sandwich fillings for next day's lunches.

Best Foods

Hellmann's Real Mayonnaise

↑IN THE WEST
←IN THE EAST

BEST FOODS≡HELLMANN'S

If You Want to Be Happy When Company Comes / 1944 / A wartime magazine advertisement for Best Foods and Hellmann's Mayonnaise, featuring a ration-based meal-extending menu including the 'super salad loaf' made of hollowed-out bologna filled with mashed peas, gelatin, and mayonnaise.

Hellmann's Mayo (branded Best on the west coast) was the first nationally distributed brand of mayo after Richard Hellmann perfected oil to salt ratios to ensure longer storage without spoilage. Hellmann's was part of an early corporate merger in the 1920's and joined with Postum Foods, which was the company name of the Kellogg Brothers (later rebranded General Foods) who manufactured peanut butter (among other things). Hellmann was a gifted marketer who originated the idea of providing recipes for his mayo and pioneered the advertising cookbook with his 'Richard Hellmann's Blue Ribbon Recipes.' Hellmann offered incentives to his workers to develop recipes; resulting in some fantastic creations like Chocolate Mayonnaise Cake and Peanut Butter & Mayo sandwiches.

Thirfty Tips on Mayonnaise Magic / c. 1940s / Laura Scudder's Farm Fresh Mayonnaise / Front and back cover / Laura Scudder was a California entrepreneurial legend. She moved to Monterey Park in 1920 with her husband Charles and took over his gas station business when he became disabled in a shop accident.

She introduced potato chips in a wax bag that included a 'made on' date to indicate freshness in 1926. This novel packaging was a hit. In the 1930s she concluded that she could keep workers employed through the economic crash of the Great Depression by expanding into peanut butter and mayonnaise production. She sold the company in 1957 to the Signal Oil & Gas Company only after they guaranteed to keep the existing work force and pay fair and living wages. She died in 1959 still at the helm of the company she founded.

The company itself was sold and resold and now exists as two brands: one owned by the Smucker's Company selling peanut butter, and an independent California company selling branded potato chips and dip mixes.

'Party Potato Salad' / Hellmann's
Mayonnaise / 1963 / Best Foods /
Magazine advertisement

'Salads in Shape for a Party' / c. 1970s /
Miracle Whip / Kraft Corporation / Miracle
Whip is not mayonnaise! Introduced at the
1933 Chicago World Fair by Kraft Foods, it
was designed as a lower-cost alternative to
mayonnaise. It contains less oil and eggs,
and more sugar and spices, than mayonnaise. The Food and Drug Administration,
which still controls the master formulary
for food products, classifies Miracle Whip
as a salad dressing.

Planters Oil
FOR FRYING · SALADS · BAKING

NEW Planters Peanut Butter

Planters DE LUXE MIXED NUTS

PLANTERS Cocktail PEANUTS

They Taste S-o-o-o Good!

® Mr. Peanut

They Taste So Good! / 1955 / Planters Peanuts /
Planters Nut and Chocolate Company / Front and back cover

Solve the Secrets of
Oriental foods

Centuries ago, the Orientals discovered the secret of browning vegetables in primitive peanut oil to bring out and accent their natural flavors. They would sometimes combine as many as nine into an irresistible one-dish flavor bouquet. Today, highly refined, quick-heating PLANTERS PEANUT OIL brings you the same wonderful secret in finer, modern, convenient form. Try these vegetable-rich casseroles to balance the family diet. Serve them Oriental style for your next daringly different party buffet.

Chow Mein Loaf (Illustrated opposite page. Serves 6)

3 cups medium white sauce (see page 16)
½ teaspoon Worcestershire sauce
2 eggs, separated
1 cup tuna fish, flaked
½ cup peanut halves
3 cups chow mein noodles

Combine 1½ cups of White Sauce with Worcestershire sauce, the 2 well beaten egg yolks, tuna, peanuts and 2 cups chow mein noodles. Beat egg whites stiffly then fold into tuna mixture and pour into well-oiled 9x5x3" loaf pan.

Bake about 30 minutes in a moderate oven (350°F) or until golden brown crust is formed.

Use: Unmold on hot platter, surrounded by remaining crisp noodles, serve with remaining 1½ cups White Sauce to which ¼ cup chopped pimento and 2 tablespoons finely chopped parsley have been added. Garnish with kumquats.

Variation: Pour into well oiled individual custard cups; bake 15–20 min.

Madras Curry (Illustrated opposite page. Serves 6)

¼ cup Planters Peanut Oil
¼ cup chopped mushrooms
⅓ cup finely chopped onions
½ cup chopped celery, cut lengthwise
⅓ cup flour
2 cups chicken broth
½ teaspoon Worcestershire sauce
½ teaspoon salt
½ teaspoon curry powder
3 cups cooked diced chicken
½ cup raisins

Heat Planters Peanut Oil in skillet, add mushrooms, onions and celery; cook until lightly browned. Blend in flour, stirring constantly. Add broth making a medium sauce, season with Worcestershire sauce, salt and curry powder. Add chicken and raisins; simmer 20 min.

Use: Serve hot over rice with chopped peanuts, chopped green pepper, sieved egg, grated cocoanut with crystallized ginger in side dishes.

Variation: ¼ cup chopped green peppers and ¼ cup chopped pimento may be added if desired.

31

They Taste So Good! / 1955 / Planters Peanuts /
Chow Mein Loaf and Madras Curry

They Taste So Good! / 1955 / Chow Mein Loaf & Madras Curry /
Planters Peanuts / Planters Nut and Chocolate Company

-and a Walnut Bowl on your table

A perfect ending for any meal!

Menu Magic
IN A NUTSHELL

branded
DIAMOND
WALNUTS
California's finest

Menu Magic In A Nutshell / 1940 / Diamond Walnuts /
Diamond Walnut Growers, Inc. / Front and back cover

Salads

Menu magicians often win their fame by some simple trick—using walnuts liberally in salads, for instance. They know that golden half kernels add appetite appeal to any salad—that a handful of crisp, crunchy, chopped kernels makes even old favorites more delectable. Try it tonight—and listen to the family cheer!

Mixed Fruit and Walnut Salad

Mixed Fruit and Walnut Salad

1 slice pineapple
12 pitted dates
1 orange
½ cup broken Diamond Walnut kernels

1 banana, sliced
2 cups seeded white grapes
Cooked salad dressing
Lettuce

Cut pineapple, dates, and pulp of orange into small pieces. Add Diamond Walnut kernels, sliced banana and grapes. Mix thoroughly. Add salad dressing to moisten and serve individually in lettuce cups or in a salad bowl, masked with additional dressing. *Serves 6.*

Christmas Salad

2 cups cranberries
2 cups granulated sugar
2 oranges
1 cup chopped Diamond Walnut kernels

1 package lime-flavored gelatin
¼ cup cold water
½ cup hot water

Grind raw cranberries fine. Add sugar and let stand for 10 minutes. Remove seeds and core from oranges and grind fine, including peel. Add oranges and Diamond Walnut kernels to cranberry mixture. Soak gelatin in cold water 5 minutes, then add hot water and stir until dissolved. Combine with fruit mixture, pour into molds which have been rinsed in cold water and chill until firm. *Serves 6 to 8.*

Walnut and Salmon Salad

2 tablespoons granu-lated gelatin
½ cup cold water
2 cups boiling water
1 teaspoon salt
½ cup granulated sugar
½ cup vinegar
2 tablespoons lemon juice

¾ cup cooked or canned salmon
¾ cup chopped cabbage
½ cup Diamond Walnut kernels
1 head lettuce
Mayonnaise or French dressing

Soak the gelatin in the cold water about 5 minutes. Add the boiling water, salt, sugar, vinegar and lemon juice, and stir until dissolved. Cool until the mixture thickens slightly, then add the salmon broken into pieces, the cabbage and Diamond Walnut kernels. Put into individual molds and chill. Serve on lettuce with mayonnaise or French dressing. *Serves 6 to 8.*

Golden Glow Salad

12 canned apricot halves
½ cup cottage cheese
⅓ cup chopped Diamond Walnut kernels
Salad dressing
12 Diamond Walnut halves

Arrange three apricot halves cut side up on each of 4 individual plates of lettuce. Combine cheese and chopped Diamond Walnut kernels, and heap in hollows of fruit. Garnish with salad dressing and Diamond Walnut halves. *Serves 4.*

Cinnamon Apples

1 cup granulated sugar
1 cup water
1 cup red cinnamon candies
6 small apples
1 cup cottage cheese

½ cup chopped Diamond Walnut kernels
2 tablespoons mayon-naise
Lettuce

Heat sugar, water, and cinnamon candies in a saucepan over a low heat until candy is dissolved. Pare and core apples, place in syrup, cover and cook very slowly until tender but not broken; the apples should be bright red. Turn once during cooking so that they will not become mushy on the bottom. Remove carefully from the syrup and chill. Fill centers with cheese, Diamond Walnut kernels and mayonnaise combined. Arrange on crisp lettuce and serve with mayonnaise if desired. *Serves 6.* These tempting, colorful salads are just as delicious as they look.

Cinnamon Apple

Jellied Fruit & Walnut Salad

1½ tablespoons granu-lated gelatin
¼ cup cold water
2 cup boiling water
½ cup granulated sugar
2 cups orange juice and pulp

½ cup chopped Diamond Walnut kernels
3 tablespoons lemon juice
Lettuce
Whipped cream
Diamond Walnut halves

Soak gelatin in cold water for 5 minutes. Add the boiling water and the sugar and stir until dissolved. Add the apple, orange, Diamond Walnut kernels and lemon juice, and combine thoroughly. Arrange in 6 individual molds which have been dipped in cold water and chill until firm. Remove from molds, and arrange on lettuce leaves. Garnish with whipped cream and Diamond Walnut halves. *Serves 6.*

Orange, Walnut, Cheese Luncheon Salad

5 or 6 oranges
24 Diamond Walnut halves
1 3-oz. package cream cheese

Lettuce
Pimiento
Salad Dressing

Pare oranges deep enough to remove every particle of membrane with the skin. Cut one orange in slices and the remaining oranges into segments. Place a large slice of orange in center of each of 4 individual lettuce-covered salad plates. Arrange around each slice 3 groups of orange segments (3 segments to a group). Moisten cheese with a little orange juice, shape into balls, and press Diamond Walnut halves into two sides. Place one of these "walnut bon-bons" between each group of orange segments and garnish slices with strips of pimiento. Serve with any dressing preferred. *Serves 4.*

Jellied Fruit & Walnut Salad

Golden Glow Salad

4

5

Menu Magic In A Nutshell / 1940 / Salads / Diamond Walnuts /
Diamond Walnut Growers, Inc.

The Cheap Cuts

➤ The butcher always knew the value of the cheaper cuts of meat. Cooking them required more work to render the fat into flavor and tenderize the muscle, but once again, home economists hired by corporations were testing new recipes and cooking methods to feed a family for the least amount of money. It may seem counterintuitive that during the heyday of wealth growth in the United States that homemakers were economizing, but the Puritanical teachings of thrift and the memory of the Great Depression kept pocketbooks closed up tight.

"Holiday Buffet"- Chicken Salad Superb, Glazed Ham Rounds, Curried Fruit Bake, Gala Corn Pudding, Parmesan-Glazed Rolls, Chocolate Torte / 1958 / *Company Meals and Buffets* / Good Housekeeping Cookbooks

Beef Beyond Belief / c. 1950s / ProTen Beef /
Swift's Premium / Front and back cover

Hamburger & Hot Dog Cookbook / 1958 / Barbequed
Franks, Frank-Stuffed Cabbage Rolls, and Frank &
Vegetable Soup / Good Housekeeping Cookbooks

Recipes for Economy Lamb Cuts With That Extra Touch / 1969 / The Lamb Council / Front cover

The Ground Meat Cookbook / 1955 / The Culinary
Arts Institute / Front and back cover

Meat Magic...
entrees with a dash
of you, added.

Lamb ala Orange
(1½.qt. casserole)

  4 shoulder lamb chops
  1 cup uncooked rice
  1 can mandarin oranges,
     drained
1½ cups beef bouillon
 ½ tsp. dried mint
Salt and pepper

Sear lamb chops briefly in
their own fat. Place uncooked
rice in buttered casserole.
Place chops over rice and
arrange oranges on top. Pour
in bouillon. Sprinkle with mint,
salt and pepper. Cover and
bake in 350-degree oven 45
minutes. Yield: 4 servings.

Mealtime Magic / 1976 / Lamb ala Orange / Anchor Hocking Glass Company

➤ Minced, forced, and chopped—red meat has been cut into little pieces and mixed with other ingredients for eons. But the American hamburger really sprung to life at the 1904 World's Fair in St. Louis (though Wisconsinites claim it was invented years before in Seymour). It's made from cheap cuts of meat and before the Food Safety Act of 1906 the source of many suspicious stories. Minces and sausages have held the public imagination as a tainted food.

World Wars I and II, using the newly accredited home economist,s began a campaign to encourage people to eat more hamburger. Meat packers agreed and from the 'teens to the fifties saw culinary innovators work their magic with ground beef. Homey casseroles and dressed-up dishes shared the tables of millions of homes across America.

Our Best Hamburger Recipes / 1957 /
Swift & Company / Front and back cover

◄ Meat Salad Mold

1 12-oz. can Luncheon Meat	2 teaspoons prepared Mustard
2 tablespoons plain Gelatin	2 teaspoons grated Onion
½ cup cold Water	½ cup chopped Celery
1½ cups Tomato Juice	½ cup chopped Sweet Pickle
3-oz. package Cream Cheese	½ cup Mayonnaise
2 tablespoons Lemon Juice	

Cut meat in ½-inch cubes. Soften gelatin in cold water. Heat tomato juice to boiling; pour over gelatin; stir until dissolved. Mash cheese; blend with lemon juice and mustard. Slowly add tomato juice mixture to cheese, stirring continuously; cool. Mix together meat, onion, celery, pickle with mayonnaise. When gelatin mixture begins to thicken, fold in meat mixture. Rinse 8-inch ring mold with cold water. Pour mixture into mold and chill until firm. If decorated mold is desired, reserve several pieces each of pickle, celery, and meat to place in mold before pouring in mixture. When ready to serve, unmold to plate and fill center with Indian Cole Slaw or Shredded Lettuce.

8-10 Servings.

23

*Appetizing Recipes From Canned Foods / c. 1930s / Meat Salad Mold /
American Can Company / The 'meat' is ground bologna.*

Variety Meats

Variety meats are available from beef, veal, pork and lamb. Each varies somewhat in flavor and tenderness; the price varies with availability and demand. Pictured here is Liver, Bacon and Onion, page 73.

Heart is good warm or cold, so cook enough for leftovers, too.

COOKED HEART

1 beef or 2 veal, lamb or pork hearts
2 tablespoons salt
¼ teaspoon powdered or 1 teaspoon leaf thyme
1 medium onion, sliced
2 to 3 tablespoons vinegar, if desired

4 TO 6 SERVINGS

Remove white tubes from heart; wash. Place in large saucepan along with remaining ingredients; cover heart with water. Bring to boil; reduce heat and simmer until tender (beef 3 to 3½ hours; pork, veal and lamb, 2 to 2½ hours). Remove heart from broth and cut into slices to serve. Or, chill and cut into thin slices.

Dress up heart with a savory stuffing. Serve with creamed corn and a colorful salad.

STUFFED HEART

1 beef heart or 2 veal hearts
4 slices bacon

Stuffing
2 cups dry bread cubes
1½ teaspoons instant minced onion
1 teaspoon salt
½ teaspoon powdered sage or thyme
Dash pepper
3 tablespoons water
2 tablespoons butter or margarine, melted

OVEN 325°   ABOUT 6 SERVINGS

Cook heart as directed for Cooked Heart (above). Meanwhile prepare stuffing. Drain heart and stuff cavity with stuffing; secure with string or skewers. Place in shallow baking dish; cover with slices of bacon. Bake, uncovered, at 325° for 40 to 45 minutes until bacon is crisp and heart is heated through. To serve, cut into slices.

Stuffing: Combine all ingredients; mix well.

Tips: If desired, use the seasoned bread cubes in the stuffing, omitting

salt and sage.
To make ahead, simmer heart, cool and refrigerate. Stuff just before baking. Bake as directed for 45 to 50 minutes.

Soup makes a quick and easy sauce for parboiled sweetbreads. Add color with a vegetable and crisp salad.

CREAMED SWEETBREADS

1½ lbs. sweetbreads
1¼ cups (10½-oz. can) condensed cream of mushroom soup
⅓ cup milk
¼ cup chopped chives or green onion
Dash Tabasco sauce

4 SERVINGS

Follow directions for parboiling sweetbreads and cleaning under Panbroiled Sweetbreads (below). Combine remaining ingredients in saucepan. Cut sweetbreads in thirds and drop into sauce. Heat and serve over buttered toast.

Sweetbreads are popular breaded and sautéed in butter. Serve with baked squash, spinach and a fruit salad.

PANBROILED SWEETBREADS

2 quarts boiling water
1 teaspoon salt
2 tablespoons vinegar or lemon juice
1½ lbs. sweetbreads
1 egg, slightly beaten
½ cup dry bread crumbs
¼ cup butter or margarine
2 tablespoons minced parsley

6 SERVINGS

In saucepan, bring water, vinegar and salt to boil. Drop in sweetbreads. Reduce heat and simmer veal and lamb sweetbreads 25 minutes; beef sweetbreads 35 minutes. Drain; rinse in cold water until cool enough to handle. Slip thin membrane off with fingers. Remove any dark veins or thick tissue. Cut sweetbreads in half. Dry thoroughly. Dip in egg, then in crumbs. Brown on both sides in butter in large fry pan. Sprinkle with parsley.

Tip: To make ahead, simmer and coat with crumbs; cool and refrigerate or freeze. Fry just before serving.

*Pillsbury's Meat Cook Book / 1969 /
Variety Meats / The Pillsbury Company*

158

"I am enclosing a recipe using your famous Boned Turkey which has proved a great favorite with my family and friends."

Mrs. Richard S. Atwood
Narragansett, R. I.

Turkey Meat Balls
SWEDISH STYLE

¼ cup minced onion
2 tablespoons finely chopped green pepper
2 tablespoons Swanson margarine or butter
1 cup fine toasted bread crumbs
½ cup milk, scalded
1 6-ounce can SWANSON BONED TURKEY, minced
1 egg

For Sauce

½ cup Swanson margarine or butter, melted
1 tablespoon Worcestershire sauce

Sauté onion and green pepper in butter until golden brown. Stir in crumbs, milk, the flavorsome turkey and egg. Mix thoroughly! Shape into tiny turkey balls. Roll in flour until well coated and fry in small amount of fat until golden brown. Place balls in top of double boiler and pour in the butter, blended with Worcestershire sauce. Cover and steam 10 to 15 minutes over boiling water and serve with fluffy rice. Makes about 40 small balls.

14

Sue Swanson's Best-loved Chicken and Turkey Recipes of 24 Good Cooks / 1948 / Turkey Meat Balls Swedish Style / Swanson Foods

Piquant Turkey Loaf
with Oyster Sauce

2 6-ounce cans SWANSON BONED TURKEY	1 beaten egg
	1 cup milk
2 cups bread cubes (2 to 3 days old)	2 tablespoons melted butter
2 tablespoons diced celery	½ teaspoon salt
2 tablespoons minced onion	¼ teaspoon pepper
½ teaspoon sage	

Mix all ingredients thoroughly, pour into well-greased loaf pan. Bake in moderate oven 350° about 1¼ hours or until golden brown and firm. Slice and serve with oyster sauce.

Oyster Sauce:

3 tablespoons butter	2 cups milk
4 tablespoons flour	1 beaten egg
¼ teaspoon salt	1 cup small oysters
¼ teaspoon celery salt	Pepper to taste

Melt butter; add flour, salt and blend to a smooth paste. Stir in milk gradually, heat to boiling, stirring constantly. Add a little hot sauce to the egg, then pour into white sauce mixture. Stir well, add oysters which have been cooked in their own juices until edges curl. (You can use canned oysters.) Add pepper.
Makes 4 to 6 servings.

17

"This recipe is my version of an old favorite at my home. Mother made it for years and we all liked it so well, but I found using Swanson Boned Turkey made an even better new favorite. Mother likes it better this way, too!"

Mrs. Usher F. Newlin, Hutchinson, Kansas

Sue Swanson's Best-loved Chicken and Turkey Recipes of 24 Good Cooks / Piquant Turkey Loaf with Oyster Sauce / 1948 / Swanson Foods

➤ Italian immigrants brought manufactured dried pasta when they came to the United States. Noodles of all sizes and shapes became the favorite of home economists and harried housewives throughout the country. Pasta was cheap and adding it to a recipe with ground meat hit all the marks as a cost-effective meal extender. Prince Pasta Company was founded in 1921 by three Sicilian immigrants to Boston. Prince quickly gained market share with their colorful cookbooks and still manufacture pasta under the American Beauty, NoYolks, and Creamette brands.

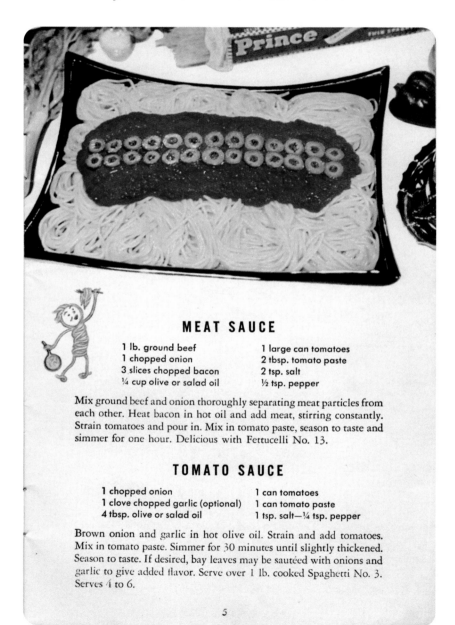

MEAT SAUCE

1 lb. ground beef	1 large can tomatoes
1 chopped onion	2 tbsp. tomato paste
3 slices chopped bacon	2 tsp. salt
¼ cup olive or salad oil	½ tsp. pepper

Mix ground beef and onion thoroughly separating meat particles from each other. Heat bacon in hot oil and add meat, stirring constantly. Strain tomatoes and pour in. Mix in tomato paste, season to taste and simmer for one hour. Delicious with Fettucelli No. 13.

TOMATO SAUCE

1 chopped onion	1 can tomatoes
1 clove chopped garlic (optional)	1 can tomato paste
4 tbsp. olive or salad oil	1 tsp. salt—¼ tsp. pepper

Brown onion and garlic in hot olive oil. Strain and add tomatoes. Mix in tomato paste. Simmer for 30 minutes until slightly thickened. Season to taste. If desired, bay leaves may be sautéed with onions and garlic to give added flavor. Serve over 1 lb. cooked Spaghetti No. 3. Serves 4 to 6.

5

Prince Golden Macaroni Recipes / 1951 /
Meat Sauce & Tomato Sauce /
Prince Macaroni Company

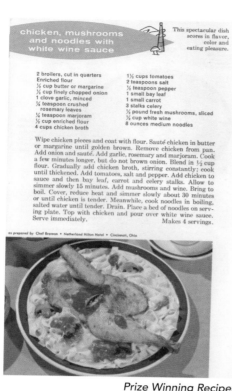

chicken, mushrooms and noodles with white wine sauce

This spectacular dish scores in flavor, color and eating pleasure.

2 broilers, cut in quarters
Enriched flour
½ cup butter or margarine
½ cup finely chopped onion
1 clove garlic, minced
¼ teaspoon crushed rosemary leaves
¼ teaspoon marjoram
½ cup enriched flour
4 cups chicken broth

1½ cups tomatoes
2 teaspoons salt
½ teaspoon pepper
1 small bay leaf
1 small carrot
3 stalks celery
½ pound fresh mushrooms, sliced
½ cup white wine
8 ounces medium noodles

Wipe chicken pieces and coat with flour. Sauté chicken in butter or margarine until golden brown. Remove chicken from pan. Add onion and sauté. Add garlic, rosemary and marjoram. Cook a few minutes longer, but do not brown onion. Blend in ½ cup flour. Gradually add chicken broth, stirring constantly; cook until thickened. Add tomatoes, salt and pepper. Add chicken to sauce and then bay leaf, carrot and celery stalks. Allow to simmer slowly 15 minutes. Add mushrooms and wine. Bring to boil. Cover, reduce heat and simmer slowly about 30 minutes or until chicken is tender. Meanwhile, cook noodles in boiling, salted water until tender. Drain. Place a bed of noodles on serving plate. Top with chicken and pour over white wine sauce. Serve immediately.   Makes 4 servings.

as prepared by Chef Brawan • Netherland Hilton Hotel • Cincinnati, Ohio

as prepared by Louise Nabell • Frances Virginia Tea Room • Atlanta, Georgia

A dish rich with shrimp, crab meat and cheese . . . a gourmet's delight.

casserole of seafood and noodles au gratin

½ cup butter or margarine
½ cup enriched flour
1 teaspoon salt
Dash pepper
4 cups milk
8 ounces medium noodles

½ pound shrimp, cooked and deveined
¾ cup flaked crab meat (6-ounce can)
½ cup sharp grated cheese
½ cup enriched bread crumbs
¼ cup melted butter or margarine

Melt butter in saucepan. Blend in flour, salt and pepper. Gradually add milk, stirring constantly; cook until sauce is thickened. Cook noodles in boiling, salted water. Drain. Place a bed of cooked noodles in 4 or 6 individual greased casseroles. On top place equal amounts of shrimp and crab meat. Cover with cream sauce. Sprinkle with cheese and top with bread crumbs. Pour melted butter over crumbs. Bake in a moderate oven (350°F.) until sauce is bubbly and crumbs are a golden brown, about 30 minutes.   Makes 4 to 6 servings.

21

Prize Winning Recipes / 1960 / Chicken, Mushrooms and Noodles with White Wine Sauce & Casserole of Seafood and Noodles Au Gratin / American Beauty Macaroni Products

as prepared by Winning S. Pendergast School Lunchrooms Detroit Public Schools Detroit, Michigan

as prepared by Gertrude Brammer • L. S. Ayres & Company • Indianapolis, Indiana

Parsley, pimiento and cheese flavor this tempting macaroni loaf. Tomato sauce is the perfect accompaniment.

macaroni loaf

¼ cup butter or margarine
¼ cup enriched flour
1 teaspoon salt
Dash pepper
Dash paprika
2 cups milk

1 egg, beaten
½ cup grated sharp cheese
1 tablespoon finely chopped pimiento
1 tablespoon finely chopped parsley
8 ounces elbow macaroni

Melt butter or margarine in saucepan. Blend in flour, salt, pepper and paprika. Gradually add milk, stirring constantly. Cook over low heat until thickened. Add a little sauce to beaten egg and blend well. Return mixture to sauce. Simmer another 3 minutes, stirring constantly. Remove from heat and stir in cheese. Add pimiento and parsley. Cook macaroni in boiling salted water until tender. Drain. Combine sauce and macaroni. Turn mixture into 8-inch square pan. Bake in moderate oven (350°F.) about 25 minutes. Serve with a tomato sauce.
Makes 4 to 6 servings.

14

A refreshing macaroni salad, accented with fruit . . . perfect with a cup of hot soup.

macaroni salad

8 ounces elbow macaroni
½ cup diced celery
3 hard-cooked eggs, chopped
3 tablespoons chopped pimiento
½ cup chopped spiced peaches or mangoes

1 tablespoon pickle relish
1 tablespoon sugar
½ teaspoon salt
1 tablespoon vinegar
½ cup mayonnaise (about)

Cook macaroni in boiling salted water until tender. Drain. Rinse in cold water and drain well. Chill. Meanwhile, combine celery, eggs, pimiento, peaches or mangoes, and pickle relish. Mix sugar and salt with vinegar and add to celery mixture. Mix in cooked macaroni. Add enough mayonnaise to moisten. Blend thoroughly.
Makes 4 to 6 servings.

15

Prize Winning Recipes / 1960 / Macaroni Loaf & Macaroni Salad / American Beauty Macaroni Products

➤ Canned tuna, salmon, and shrimp were a low-cost protein championed by home economists. Never one to miss a marketing opportunity, every food processor soon published recipes containing the fish. The age of the tuna casserole was upon us.

Good Housekeeping's Book of Salads / 1958 / Shrimp Green Goddess
Salad, Tuna Fruit Buffet Salad, Tangy Ham Mold, His & Hers Crab Salad /
Good Housekeeping Books

Seafood Magic...a new catch of ideas, plus some personal presto.

Shrimp Petites (Illustrated)
(4-10 oz. deep pie dishes)

1½ lbs. frozen shrimp,
    thawed, drained
2 tbs. butter
2 tbs. flour
1¼ cups light cream
Salt and pepper to taste
⅓ cup catsup
Tiny pinch of nutmeg
Bread crumbs

Melt butter, blend in flour. Add cream slowly, with salt and pepper. Cook until thickened. Stir in catsup and nutmeg. Add shrimp and pour into buttered baking dishes. Sprinkle with crumbs. Bake in 325-degree oven 20 to 25 minutes. Yield: 4 servings.

Mealtime Magic / 1976 / Shrimp Petites / Anchor Hocking Glass Company

164

Medley of Meats / 1977 / Tuna Piquant / Favorite Recipe Press / Favorite Recipe Press is a specialty publisher that produces fundraising and custom advertising cookbooks. An organization or business can purchase a 'stock' cookbook and brand it with their logo. It follows in the long tradition of popular recipes duplicated and shared in many cookbooks with little attribution.

Depression and War

➤ Good marketing responds to current events while creating optimism for consumers. The Great Depression of the 1930s brought out collectivism from food companies that is reflected in their cookbooks. Money-saving and meal-stretching with a focus on getting enough calories and nutrition from food was a prevailing theme.

As the Depression ended and War World II began, food producers quickly adjusted recipes from cost-saving to rationing as they experimented with substitute ingredients, home-grown vegetables, and flavor-boosting products. Casseroles, hotpots, and prepare-ahead meals were highlighted as many women joined the workforce to take on the jobs left behind by soldiers, sailors, and marines.

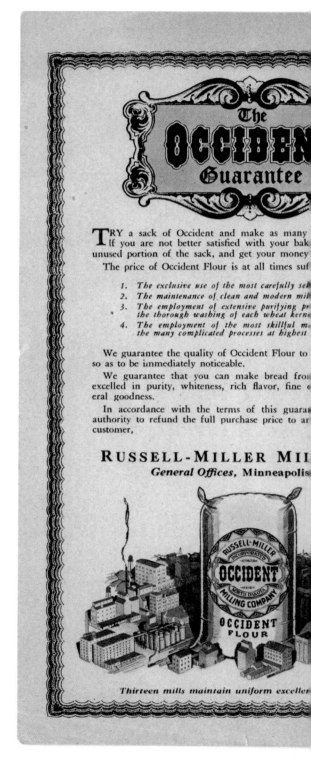

Occident Flour Cookbook / 1934 / Russell-Miller Milling Company / Front and back cover / Note that the logo of the NRA (National Recovery Administration) is proudly placed on the cover that told consumers the company followed the NRA regulations of fair pricing, fair wages, and fair working hours. The short-lived NRA was abolished in late 1935 when the Supreme Court declared the law that established the agency was unconstitutional.

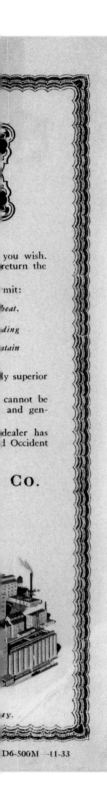

Dear Madam:

Baking is easy with Occident Flour. You are assured of perfect results always.

Watch the popularity of your bread plate grow when you bake with Occident. Watch, too, how much longer your baking holds oven-fresh flavor.

The following pages contain a variety of recipes developed and tested in our own Home Economics Kitchen. We know you will enjoy using them. If you would like to have additional recipes, we shall be glad to supply them.

Please use Occident Flour with these recipes. You will have uniformly perfect results every time, if ingredients are measured accurately, if you follow the method given — and you use Occident Flour.

Yours for better baking

Russell-Miller Milling Co.

What You Can Do with One Pound of Hamburger / 1943 / Better Homemaking Institute / Front cover / Also note the racist chef in blackface cartoon price sticker in the lower right corner.

GRACE VIALL GRAY   BETTY GAY

Foreword

Dear American Homemakers:

The menus and recipes in this booklet have been developed in the kitchens of Better Homemaking Institute and Food Research Corporation.

Thousands of homemakers come to our institute yearly for instructions in the art of homemaking. We have learned from these homemakers their greatest needs. We have found that they want inexpensive, yet nutritious foods with which to feed their families.

These homemakers have approved the menus and recipes contained in this booklet, and so it is in the spirit of helpfulness that we are passing them on to you homemakers everywhere.

The homemaker of today is an extremely busy woman, with little time for menu planning and cooking. We have therefore endeavored to give her simple, easily prepared menus.

We hope you will enjoy our meals and recipes as much as we did preparing them for you.

Cordially yours,

Grace Viall Gray
Betty Gay

SUNDAY DINNER MENU

*Hamburger Ring Filled with Mashed Potatoes
Broiled Tomatoes and Mushrooms
Shredded Raw Carrot and Celery Salad
French Bread   Butter

Upside-Down Cake
Coffee or Tea

HAMBURGER RING
(Serves 6 to 8)

1 pound hamburger	2 tablespoons chopped green
½ pound ground pork	pepper
2 tablespoons grated onion	1 egg
2 tablespoons prepared	1 cup fine cracker crumbs
horseradish	¾ cup milk
1 teaspoon salt	¼ cup catsup, if desired
1 teaspoon prepared mustard	

Combine meat and remaining ingredients except catsup. Mix well. Grease a ring mold—put catsup in bottom. Pack meat mixture into mold and place in a pan of hot water. Bake in a moderately hot oven (375°F.), for about 1¼ hours.

SERVING SUGGESTIONS: Unmold baked ring on a large chop plate. Fill center with mashed potatoes. Sprinkle with paprika. Arrange broiled tomatoes around outside of mold, topping each with broiled mushrooms. Garnish with parsley.

3

*What You Can Do with One Pound of Hamburger / 1943 /
Foreword and Sunday Dinner Menu / Better Homemaking Institute*

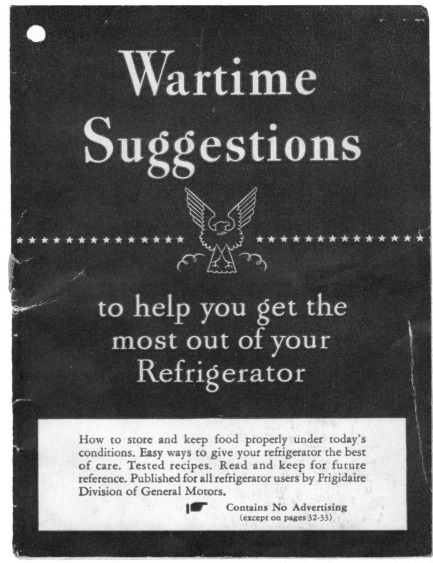

Wartime Suggestions / 1943 /
Frigidaire Division of General Motors / Front cover

Recipes
for Today

Recipes for Today / 1943 / General Foods Corporation /
Front cover / General Foods introduced a wartime spokeswoman (in cartoon form) to market their products with a
patriotic spin. Victorianna is the niece of Uncle Sam and
worked to remind consumers of their obligation to conserve food for the war effort.

Food Will Win The War And Write The Peace / 1943 / Kerr Glass Manufacturing Corporation / Front cover / Home food preservation was the next logical step for Victory Gardens, and the federal government supported Kerr and Ball Company in their efforts to teach and encourage Americans to preserve their harvests.

— AND I'M NO PART-TIME WIFE!

It's up to me to keep my family fit with nutritious foods

Include in your daily menus "fitness foods"—that is our Nutritional Authorities' plea to every homemaker in America. High among these stand the whole grain foods. And the refreshing, nut-like flavor of Nabisco Shredded Wheat—100% whole wheat in its most delicious form—makes it mighty easy to follow this important rule of nutrition. Here, too, is a good source of Vitamin B_1 as *Nature* provides it.

OUR HOME FRONT lies in the kitchens of American homes. When breakfast is built around Nabisco Shredded Wheat (with milk and peaches or other fruit), it brings better days for every one. Ask for it by the *full name*—Nabisco Shredded Wheat.

CHILDREN, TOO, CAN HELP. And they, also, need energy foods. Nabisco Shredded Wheat gives all of whole wheat's energy. It is, as well, a good source of Vitamin B_1 as *Nature* provides it—the vitamin that converts food into energy.

A good source of Vitamin B_1 as *Nature* provides it

U.S. NEEDS US STRONG

THIS TYPE OF FOOD IS AMONG THOSE RECOMMENDED IN THE NUTRITION FOOD RULES

EAT NUTRITIONAL FOOD

NABISCO SHREDDED WHEAT

Baked by NABISCO . . . NATIONAL BISCUIT COMPANY

'And I'm No Part-Time Wife' / 1943 / Shredded Wheat / Nabisco / Magazine advertisement stressing the important role that women played in keeping the family healthy and working while serving her country; the Puritan ethics of the 1600s were still the cultural norm.

➤ As the war kept on, corporations used advertising as morale boosters while indulging in the worst of racial fearmongering.

Paper shortages and manufacturing for the war effort reduced the overall number of advertising cookbooks produced from 1940 to 1945. American lend-lease programs instituted by FDR to assist British and Russian allies meant that the United States was producing war machines, processing food, and had adopted a war economy since 1939.

"Breakfast of Champions" / 1944 / General Mills / Magazine advertisement series / Drawn by prolific illustrator and cartoonist Dave Gerard, the series features a squad of 'everyman' marines in the Pacific theater using anti-Japanese language while they talk about Wheaties.

Food Sells Everything

➤ By the late 1960s and early 1970s advertisers couldn't resist cookbooks. Companies devised ways to use their products in recipes. Galliano enjoyed its peak in popularity when this 1972 cookbook recommended marinating a beef roast while drinking a cocktail then enjoying a Galliano-flambéed crepes. Regnier never imagined inestimable teenage hangovers when they introduced Sloe Gin to the United States; the Sloe Sweet Potato Pie never reached the heights of popularity of the Sloe Gin Fizz.

Soda pop companies too had recommendations for cooking. Dr Pepper had a recipe for every type of meal including the now iconic Soda Pop Chicken.

Structured to keep the plot low in calories: Melon Cup and Strawberry Bavarian with Special Whipped Topping (P. 12).

Designed and produced by
Western Printing and Lithographing Company
All photographs by Foster Ensminger

Dr Pepper and Diet Dr Pepper are registered trademarks of Dr Pepper Company.

Cookin' With Dr. Pepper / 1965 / Dr. Pepper Company / Front and back covers

Galliano Pot Roast / 1972 /
Cordial Accents / Regnier Corporation

DESSERTS

Galliano Crepes / 1972 /
Cordial Accents / Regnier Corporation

Sloe Gin

Drinks

Sloe Libre

¼ lime   Cola
1½ oz. Regnier Sloe
   Gin

Squeeze the lime and drop into tall glass over ice cubes. Add Sloe Gin; stir. Add Cola to fill.

Sloe Gin Cup

1 slice lemon   1½ oz. Regnier
Thin, long cucumber   Sloe Gin
  wedge, unpeeled Tom Collins Mix

Place lemon and cucumber wedge in tall glass with ice. Add Sloe Gin, fill with Collins mix. Stir with cucumber.

Sloe Gin Fizz

1½ oz. Regnier   2 oz. lemon juice
  Sloe Gin   Soda
¾ oz. bar syrup

Shake Sloe Gin, bar syrup, lemon juice, with cracked ice. Strain into Fizz glass, top with soda.

Sloe Gin Rickey

1½ oz. Regnier   Soda
  Sloe Gin

Squeeze lime over ice cubes in tall glass; drop into glass. Add Sloe Gin, stir, fill with soda.

Entrées

Duckling Regnier

1 duckling, 5 lbs.   2 celery stalks,
Salt, pepper, ginger   with leaves
2 cloves garlic, mashed ½ cup white wine
1 whole orange,   2 oz. Regnier Sloe Gin
  quartered

Season duckling inside and out with spices and garlic. Put orange quarters and celery into cavity. Roast in a preheated 325°F. oven, about 1½ hours, basting frequently with wine and Sloe Gin.

Sloe Gin Glaze

1 oz. Regnier Sloe Gin 1 tablespoon lemon juice
2 tablespoons honey   Pinch ginger

Skim fat from pan drippings, blend drippings with Sloe Gin and other glaze ingredients. Baste duck with glaze and continue roasting about 1 hour until duck is very tender. Makes 4 servings.

To Blaze

2 oz. Regnier Sloe Gin

Heat Sloe Gin in a ladle or small pan, ignite, pour over duck.
TIP: Use the same glaze for roast turkey prepared your favorite way, doubling the glaze ingredients.

Desserts

Sloe Sweet Potato Pie

2 cups mashed sweet ¼ teaspoon powdered
  potatoes, fresh-cooked   cloves
  or vacuum-packed 3 eggs, beaten
3 tablespoons Regnier ¼ cup melted butter
  Sloe Gin   1 cup milk
½ cup sugar   Pastry-lined
½ teaspoon salt   9-inch pie plate
¼ teaspoon cinnamon

Combine potatoes with Sloe Gin and other ingredients, beat well. Pour into pie plate, bake at (450°F.) about 10 minutes, at (350°F.) about 40 minutes longer, until crust is golden and a silver knife inserted near the center of the pie comes out clean.

Sloe Gin Crock

1 can (1 lb.) pineapple ½ cup grapes
  or other fruit,   ½ cup strawberries
  drained   1½ cups sugar
2 fresh pears or   2 cups Regnier Sloe Gin
  peaches, in wedges

Combine cut fruits or arrange in 4-cup container in attractive pattern, alternately with sugar. Add Sloe Gin. Cover, let stand 1 week or longer. Makes 6-8 servings.

Sloe plums from France combine with American cherries to make Regnier's Sloe Gin a joyous addition to your table. Say "Ray-niay."

Sloe Gin / 1972 /
Cordial Accents / Regnier Corporation

➤ Businesses with tenuous relationships with food created cookbooks that reflected their corporate culture. Breweries focused on types of cooking acceptable to men—grilling, bar-b-q, and meats, while the Remington Arms cookbook is solely about preparing wild game. Troy-Bilt, International Harvester, and John Deere published books in the 1970s that harkened back to a nostalgic and disappearing rural lifestyle and farm foods.

The Sportsman's Way / 1949 / A. Gettleman
Brewing Company / Front cover

Troy-Bilt Tiller Owner's Recipe Collection #1 / 1976 /
Garden Way Manufacturing Company, Inc.

➤ Cooking tools and appliances heavily invested in teaching people how to cook with their newest gadgets. Refrigerators, stoves, electric griddles, and even glass bakeware were all occasion for a new cookbook.

How To Dress, Ship, and Cook Wild Game / 1951 / Remington Arms Company / Front cover

Mealtime Magic / 1976 / Anchor Hocking / Front cover

Chuckwagon Cooking from Marlboro Country / 1981 /
Philip Morris, Inc. / Front cover

➤ The Antisocial Cookbook is a triumph of marketing genius. Published in 1968 by the Binaca breath spray company, the book features recipes loaded with ingredients like onions, garlic, fish, and more, that ensure lousy breath.

The Antisocial Cookbook / 1968 /
BINACA / Madison Labratories / Front cover

Sweet Treats

➤ Cakes, cookies, pies, puddings…corporations invented the 'sweet tooth.' Our bodies crave the simple carbohydrates of sugar because of the energy bang it delivers, but it was a rare find in the pre-industrialized world.

A Calendar of Desserts / 1940 /
General Foods / Multiple brands / Front cover

A Calendar of Desserts / 1940 /
General Foods / Multiple brands / Back cover

> The single quantifiable change to the Western diet from the 1900s to the present day is the increase in our sugar consumption. It's been common practice to blame willpower, weakness, and laziness for our obesity crisis but science says otherwise. Studies across the board for the past 50 years have shown that though our average overall caloric consumption and usage has remained the same, the percentage of those calories derived from sugar has increased a hundredfold. We're not eating more candy, but we are eating more processed foods.

The Swans Down Cake
Manual / 1933 / Reily
Foods Company /
Front and back cover

Sugars were rare in the pre-agricultural communities where we once lived, and our bodies and brains evolved to consume as much of the delicacy whenever we encountered it. Sugar literally triggers our brains to eat more food. Companies have spent millions of dollars figuring out ways to get more sugar and salt into our food. Make no mistake, all modern processed foods have added sugars. But before we arrived at sugared everything, companies focused on convincing housewives that no meal was complete unless dessert was served.

New Fashioned Old Fashioned Recipes / 1949 /
Arm & Hammer and Cow Brand Baking Soda /
Church & Dwight / Front cover

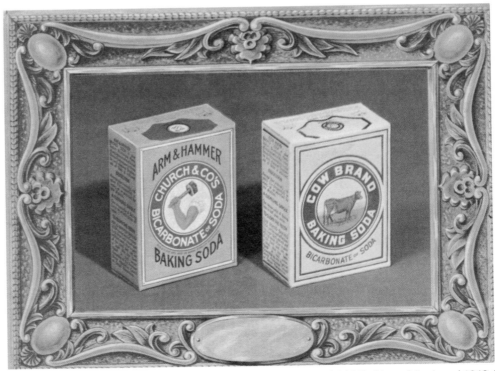

New Fashioned Old Fashioned Recipes / 1949 /
Arm & Hammer and Cow Brand Baking Soda /
Church & Dwight / Back cover

Party Bait / 1954 / Nestle's Semi-Sweet
Baking Morsels / Nestle Company /
Front cover

Sweet Treats - Recipes from Nestle / 1969 /
Nestle Company / Front and back cover

➤ Yes, cheese has been made by humans for thousands of years, but the cream-enriched non-aged cheeses inspired by European boursin and mascarpone styles began their commercial life in 1880 when 'Philadelphia Cream Cheese' was mass-produced in a New York Factory. (The Philadelphia in the name denotes a style of cheese made by homemakers and dairy farms in the region.) Typical Philly cream cheese has 33% milkfats, and carrageenan thickeners. Cookbooks from the early 1800s show recipes for making cream cheese at home but the dawn of the 1900s when competing cream cheese manufacturers began developing recipes both sweet and savory, saw its popularity rise as the go-to ingredient for everything from pies to Crab Rangoon.

Our consumption of dairy changed with the cultivation of sugar. A large percentage of American sugar consumption comes from processed dairy foods like yogurts, cheeses, and ice cream, and as shown here—dairy-rich desserts.

New and entertaining ideas all from a cream cheese / c. 1930s / Tomato Rose Salad and Lemon Cream Cheese Tarts / Philadelphia Cream Cheese / Kraft Foods, Inc.

STRAWBERRY CREAM CHEESE PIE

½-lb. pkg. Philadelphia Brand Cream Cheese

2 tablespoons milk

1 baked 9″ pie shell

1 qt. fresh strawberries

¾ cup sugar

2 tablespoons cornstarch

⅛ cup water

Few drops of red food coloring

Blend together the cream cheese and milk; whip fluffy. Spread half of mixture on the bottom of pie shell. Top with half of strawberries. Cut remaining berries in half. Combine sugar, cornstarch, water. Add remaining strawberries and cook until thickened, stirring constantly. Add red food coloring; mix well. Pour into pie shell. Chill, decorate with remaining cream cheese.

CHOCOLATE "PHILLY" NUGGETS

3-oz. pkg. Philadelphia Brand Cream Cheese

2 cups sifted confectioners' sugar

2 1-oz. squares unsweetened chocolate, melted

¼ teaspoon vanilla

Dash of salt

Pecan halves

Place cream cheese in a bowl and cream until soft and smooth. Slowly blend sugar into it. Add melted chocolate. Mix well. Add vanilla and salt and mix until well blended. Form into nuggets, using 1 tablespoon of mixture for each. Press a pecan half into top of each nugget. Place in refrigerator until firm (about 15 minutes).

COCONUT "PHILLY" BONBONS

3-oz. pkg. Philadelphia Brand Cream Cheese

2½ cups sifted confectioners' sugar

¼ teaspoon vanilla

Dash of salt

* * *

Shredded coconut

Place cream cheese in bowl and cream until soft and smooth; slowly blend in sugar. Add vanilla and salt; mix until well blended. Form into balls, using 1 tablespoon of mixture for each. Roll in coconut; chill until firm.

JELLIED CUCUMBER SALAD

1 envelope gelatin

½ cup cold water

½ cup boiling water

2 cups finely shredded cucumber

1 tablespoon lemon juice

1 tablespoon vinegar

1 teaspoon salt

3-oz. pkg. Philadelphia Brand Cream Cheese

Milk

Watercress

Soften gelatin in cold water; dissolve in boiling water. Add cucumber, lemon juice, vinegar and salt. Chill until slightly thickened. Pour into a fancy 1-qt. mold and chill until firm. Unmold and garnish with cream cheese which has been whipped with a small amount of milk and forced through a pastry tube. Surround with watercress.

New and entertaining ideas all from a cream cheese / c. 1930s / Strawberry Cream Cheese Pie, Chocolate "Philly" Nuggets, Coconut "Philly" Bon Bons, and Jellied Cucumber Salad / Philadelphia Cream Cheese / Kraft Foods, Inc.

Knudsen Recipes for Greater Food Value / 1957 / Knudsen Dairy Products / Front cover

68 treasured Holiday Recipes from Land O'Lakes.

Only love beats butter

Turkey baking ideas. Glazes. Stuffings. Appetizers. Holiday breads, desserts, cakes, pies, cookies, candies. And more.

Only Love Beats Butter / 1977 / Land O' Lakes, Inc. / Front cover / Land O' Lakes is a Minnesota-based cooperative cooperation founded in 1921 and comprised of over 1000 farmer and producer members. It is the third largest co-op in the United States.

The Experts

➤ Edward Bernays, Freud's nephew, trained in the scientific art of psychoanalysis, made 'appealing to expertise' a cornerstone of advertising. His research showed that consumers respond to endorsements by doctors, celebrities, and in the case of food, the growing army of Home Economists. Companies hired experts from cooking schools and local radio programs who then developed recipes using their products.

Sunkist Juniorette
Electric
JUICE
EXTRACTOR

Fresh orange juice has become a standard part of any and every meal—and for between-meals refreshment. Beverages made with fresh lemon juice are also widely popular.

There's a secret, however, in preparing these fruit beverages. Like coffee or tea, they should always be served fresh. Juice that stands for even a short time loses flavor.

To make it easy for you to prepare orange and lemon juice quickly whenever you want

and operated *Sunkist* ilies of one or two ments) and *Su* larger families tors are switch an against r every bit

FOR VIGOROUS HEALTH -

SUNKIST RECIPES
for Every Day

kist Junior
Electric
**JUICE
XTRACTOR**

it, Sunkist
ponsors three
ghly efficient
ne extracting
ices, on sale
where: The
t Reamer
hite, green,
ily operated
e electrically
te (for fam-
mall apart-
unior (for
atter extrac-
perate. Flip
alved fruit
lb. Extracts

*For Vigorous Health - Sunkist Recipes for Every Day / 1935 /
California Fruit Growers Exchange / Front and back cover*

Food value of Citrus Fruits

ORANGES and lemons are valuable and necessary parts of the well-balanced diet because:

1. They aid digestion.
2. They supply vital food elements that counteract tooth decay and gum troubles.
3. They prevent and correct acidosis.
4. They promote the retention of calcium and phosphorus.
5. They furnish laxative bulk of the best type.
6. They stimulate growth in children.

Lazy Daisy Salad

These beneficial results are partially due to the fact that oranges and lemons contribute to the diet:

1. *Vitamins:* The protective food elements necessary for health and proper growth. These fruits contain Vitamins A, B and C, being particularly rich in Vitamin C. This vitamin is readily destroyed by heat in cooked foods. Oranges, lemons and grapefruit supply it in an uncooked and easily secured form. Because Vitamin C cannot be stored in the body, some food containing it should be eaten daily.
2. *Alkaline Salts:* Which leave an alkaline-ash in the process of digestion. They are valuable in balancing the acid of other good and necessary but acid-ash foods, such as meats, eggs, fish, fowl, breads and cereals.
3. *Minerals:* That build strong bones and teeth, rich blood, nerve tissue and help to regulate the body. Oranges contain calcium, phosphorus and iron.
4. *Fruit Sugar:* Furnishing quick energy. A large orange will supply 100 calories. The sugar in an orange is very easily digested and oranges furnish a healthful form of sweets for between-meal lunches.
5. *Fruit Acids:* These give oranges and lemons their delicious, refreshing flavor and stimulate the appetite. Thus they also aid digestion and are slightly laxative in effect.
6. *Cellulose:* Cellulose is valuable for its laxative effect.
7. *Water:* Mother Nature has bottled pure water in oranges, lemons and grapefruit in germ-proof containers. Fresh fruit drinks made from these fruits are better than artificial beverages.

For more complete information about the nutritional and healthful qualities of Sunkist oranges and lemons, write for free health booklet, "Fruits That Help Keep the Body Vigorous," addressing: California Fruit Growers Exchange, Box 530, Station C, Los Angeles, California.

2

Preparation of Fruit

PREPARATION OF ORANGES FOR SALAD AND DESSERT USES

SUNKIST oranges have special value for salad and dessert uses. In addition to excellence of flavor, they are practically free from seeds and have a firm meat, easy to prepare in the slices and segments used for these dishes. Large or medium size fruit segments well, small fruit slices better.

Segments: With a sharp knife, peel down to juicy meat, removing all outer skin and membrane. Cut on either side of each dividing membrane and remove meat, segment by segment.

Slices: Peel fruit down to juicy pulp. Cut in thin, even slices. Slices may be halved or quartered for easier handling.

Pieces: Cut segments or slices in pieces.

Shells: Attractive baskets for the serving of fruit cups, salads and desserts are also made from the clean, waxy-textured skins of Sunkist oranges. . . (See directions, page 21.)

Note: Save any escaping juice in preparing segments or slices and use for salad dressings and marinades. . . (See pages 24-25.)

JUICE PREPARATION

See Orange Juice, page 26.

BREAKFAST PREPARATION

Arrange Sunkist orange slices or segments on plates in attractive design, sweetening, if desired, with honey or maple syrup.

FLAVOR USES OF PEEL

Grated orange and lemon rind are used by the best cooks to flavor cakes, pies, breads, desserts, frostings, fillings and sauces, being preferred for flavor and economy to commercially prepared extracts.

In grating, only the yellow portion of the rind should be removed. This yellow portion contains the oil cells from which come the oils that give flavor.

Sunkist oranges and lemons have clean skins of waxy texture, especially suited for grated rind and ground peel.

Grated Peels: Grate only the yellow portion. Use fresh or mix with sugar and keep in a tightly covered jar.

Ground Peels: The whole peel may be ground fine and used like grated rind.

Candied Peels: See page 8.

Peeling	Segmenting	Slicing

3

For Vigorous Health - Sunkist Recipes for Every Day / 1935 /
Food Values of Citrus Fruits & Preparation of Fruit /
California Fruit Growers Exchange

Menu Planning for Good Nutrition

The knowledge of the facts for good nutrition without the application will reap no reward. To produce and maintain good health, daily menus should include:

EGGS

One each day per person—or at least 3 to 4 a week.

Eggs may be served plain as poached, scrambled, hard-cooked, or in an omelet; in cooking as soufflés, custards, sauces, breads or cakes and salads.

LEAN MEAT, POULTRY OR FISH

One or more servings daily (Fresh or Canned)

Different kinds of meat, poultry and fish are necessary for variety of food value and flavor. The many canned meats, poultry and fish available make nutritious meals quick and easy to prepare. Include occasionally among the meat dishes on your menus, liver, kidney, salmon, sardines, tuna, herring or mackerel.

CEREALS, BREADS, AND FLOUR

A cereal every day.

At least 2 servings of whole grain or enriched white bread.

Whole grain, restored or enriched cereals are important in everyday meals; use ready-to-eat or cooked, for breakfast with milk and fruit, in cookies, puddings or in meat and fish loaves. Serve creamed dishes on toast; make bread stuffings and puddings. Use enriched white flour in home made breads, gravies and sauces.

FATS

Two or more tablespoons butter or vitamin-fortified margarine. Count salt pork or bacon as a fat.

FRUITS

One citrus fruit or juice — or tomato juice
One other fruit (Canned or Fresh)

Canned juices and fruits also offer an economical variety to the menu and can be included easily and quickly to "pep up" appetites.

MILK

One quart for each child. One pint for each adult. (Fresh or Evaporated)

Count one pint of undiluted evaporated milk (a little more than one tall can) or ¼ pound of dry milk—or 1/3 pound of cheese as having about the same food value as one quart of fluid milk. For variety, include milk in your cooked foods, such as soups, creamed or scalloped dishes, ice creams, custards or other milk desserts. For variety, include cheese, buttermilk, malted and chocolate milks in your menus.

VEGETABLES

Three or more each day (Canned or Fresh)
One green, leafy or yellow vegetable. One other vegetable. One potato

Canned vegetables offer the necessary variety to your menus. There is no waste to canned vegetables; the entire contents of the can should be used. It is wise to include one raw vegetable each day, especially salad greens.

SWEETS

Use molasses, syrups, honey, jellies, jams, desserts and candies in moderation to make the diet palatable but not enough to spoil the appetite for other foods.

However, meals need not be humdrum. Make them interesting, colorful and attractive. Vary the preparation of the foods you use; vary the manner in which you serve them. Include appealing, nutritious recipes. Your family will eat the foods which are good for them and at the same time enjoy them.

2

Using Commercially Canned Foods

Canned Foods are delicious just as they come from the can. Remember that canned foods are cooked foods. When heating commercially canned vegetables follow these directions:

1. *Drain the liquid into a saucepan.*
2. *Boil it quickly to reduce the amount.*
3. *Add the vegetable and heat quickly.*
4. *Season to the family's taste and serve.*

Instead of reducing the liquid in the can, it may be saved for soups, sauces, gravies or vegetable cocktails. Do *not* throw it away as it contains valuable nutrients.

Many women like to use canned foods as an ingredient of interesting recipes. The canner has done the first hard work of preparation, so it is easy to add variety to the menu with very little effort.

FACTS TO REMEMBER ABOUT COMMERCIALLY CANNED FOODS:

1. Fruits and vegetables used for canning are especially grown for that purpose; picked at just the right point of maturity, sealed in cans and cooked in the briefest possible time after harvesting.

2. Nothing is added to canned fruits except a sugar syrup; and nothing to canned vegetables except water and sometimes a little salt or sugar for seasoning.

3. The canning process does not affect the food value of the starches, sugars, fats and proteins. The canning industry has developed many methods designed to conserve the vitamins and minerals of the fresh raw products. Hence, modern commercially canned foods retain in good degree the food values of the fresh foods used for canning.

4. Canned Food may be safely left in the open can if it is covered and kept in a refrigerator. This you should do with left-over cooked food stored in any type of container.

5. The use of commercially canned foods saves many hours of preparation of raw fruits, vegetables, fish and meats, and also assures no waste.

3

Appetizing Recipes from Canned Foods / 1930 /
Menu Planning for Good Nutrition & Using Commercially
Canned Foods / American Can Company

198

➤ New food products meant that experts were needed to teach people how to use them correctly. Advertising cookbooks that combined health and nutrition information with actual instructions for use were a standard way to introduce a new food. Even now, though the medium has changed, consumers are inundated with quick-speed videos demonstrating ways to eat everything from pomegranates to crickets.

The Sealtest Food Advisor for Spring 1938 / 1938 / Sealtest Dairy / Front cover

> 'Sue Swanson' was the invented spokeswoman for Swanson Frozen Foods, inventor, and innovator of that icon of mid-century American cuisine, the TV Dinner. The mysterious 'Jane Ashley' only appears to have created recipes for the Corn Producers Association. But Martha Lee Anderson (staff home economist for Dwight & Church Company) was a real woman who represented the true expertise as handed down by generations of 'scientific cooking' teachers.

This little cook book is dedicated to you who would like to give your families more of your homemade good things, if you only had the time.

Bisquick makes that possible ...good homemade food, quickly prepared. You can cook with love and enjoy the cooking more, when you use this cook book and your Bisquick. Once you start, I know you'll want to try every idea in the book.

Betty Crocker

CONTENTS

2

Betty Crocker's Bisquick Cook Book / 1959 / Table of contents / General Mills / "Betty Crocker" is fictional.

➤ In the case of 'Betty Crocker,' she was created in 1921 by the Washburn-Crosby Company (which later morphed into General Mills) to be the friendly expert dispensing advice and recipes. Like Aunt Jemima, she was portrayed on the radio by a series of actresses until the jig was up with the advent of television. A composite image of a kindly, middle-aged white woman graced the packaging for years until General Mills replaced the image of Betty with a red spoon bearing the name 'Betty Crocker' instead.

Betty Crocker's Bisquick Cook Book / 1956 / General Mills Inc. / Front and back cover / "Betty Crocker" was a fictional character.

Cooking with Condensed Soups / 1950 / Campbell's Soup Company / Front and back cover / "Anne Marshall" was a fictional character.

Some of my Favorite
Good Things to Eat

THIS collection of recipes offers real treats for you and your family.

Many favorite recipes call for sour milk, but if it is not available, you may easily make it.

A SUBSTITUTE FOR SOUR MILK: Simply place 4 teaspoons lemon juice or vinegar in a standard measuring cup, then fill to the 1 cup mark with sweet milk or diluted evaporated milk. The resulting liquid is equal to natural sour milk or buttermilk when they are best for baking. White vinegar makes a whiter product than brown vinegar.

Sour cream may similarly be made by using sweet cream with vinegar or lemon juice.

Arm & Hammer Brand Baking Soda and Cow Brand Baking Soda meet all the requirements of the United States Pharmacopoeia. Both are pure bicarbonate of soda and can be used wherever bicarbonate of soda is prescribed.

Martha Lee Anderson

2

Research Test Kitchen
Church & Dwight Co., Inc.
Syracuse, N. Y.

EDITION 123 COPYRIGHT 1940 BY CHURCH & DWIGHT CO., INC., 10 CEDAR ST., NEW YORK, N.Y.

Some of My Favorite Good Things to Eat / 1940 /
Interior cover / Arm & Hammer brand / Church & Dwight
Company, Inc. / "Martha Lee Anderson"
was a fictional character.

Jane Ashley's Newest Recipes for Better Meals / 1952 / Karo, Mazola,
Argo, Kre-Mel, and Niagra brands / Corn Products Refining Company /
Front cover / "Jane Ashley" was a fictional character.

10¢

Best-loved Chicken and Turkey Recipes of 24 Good Cooks

collected by Sue Swanson

Sue Swanson's Best-loved Chicken and Turkey Recipes of 24 Good Cooks / 1948 /
Front cover / Swanson Company / "Sue Swanson" was a fictional character.

Hello!

One of the things I like best about cooking is swapping recipes. I think most of you agree, for lately I've been asking homemakers to share with me their favorite ways of using our Swanson canned chicken and turkey products—and the response has been tremendous.

Here are just a few of the extra-choice dishes that have been sent from all parts of the country. I hope to share many more of these recipes with you later.

Our Swanson canned chicken and turkey products are delicious used just as they come from the can. But nowadays, homemakers delight in trying new things and in finding new ways to serve the faithful stand-bys. So if you have a new, unusual recipe using Swanson canned chicken or turkey, do send it to me.

If yours is a truly original recipe and we decide to use it in our advertising or publish it in any way, we will mail you a check for $25 just as we did for these.

Mail your recipe with complete directions to me: Sue Swanson, Box 1652, Dept. RB-1, Omaha, Nebraska.

I hope you will find this little booklet interesting and useful!

Sincerely,
Sue Swanson

Sue Swanson's Best-loved Chicken and Turkey Recipes of 24 Good Cooks / 1948 /
Hello! & Table of Contents / Swanson Company / "Sue Swanson" was a fictional character.

➤ Readers of *Good Housekeeping, Ladies Home Journal,* and their sisters often wrote in asking for and giving advice to fellow readers. Food producers took this cultural movement of self-taught expertise and turned it into a competition. The Pillsbury Bake-Off is still going strong today with cooks developing recipes to win both prizes and accolades. We see this idea alive today in the popular amateur cooking competition television programs.

King Midas Baking Queens Favorite Recipes / 1962 /
King Midas Flour / Midas Mills / Front cover

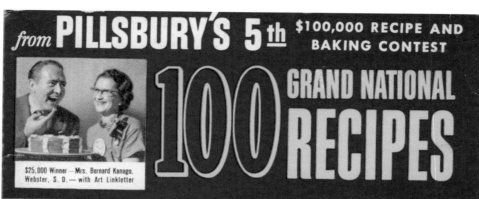

NEW!
1954
GRAND NATIONAL
RECIPE BOOK
25¢

Easy-to-follow Prize Winning Recipes

100 Grand National Recipes / 1954 / Pillsbury Mills, Inc. / Front cover

Fork 'N' Finger Onion Pie
by Mrs. H. Goehl, Morris Plains, New Jersey

Crust

1½ cups Pillsbury's Best All Purpose
   Flour*
½ cup Pillsbury Hungry Jack Mashed
   Potato Flakes
½ teaspoon soda
½ teaspoon salt
½ teaspoon garlic salt
½ cup butter
⅓ cup dairy sour cream
6 strips crisp bacon, crumbled

Filling

4 eggs, slightly beaten
1⅔ cups dairy sour cream
1 cup shredded Cheddar cheese
1 jar (2 oz.) pimiento, drained and
   finely chopped
1 teaspoon caraway seed
1 envelope (1⅜ oz.) onion soup mix

OVEN 375°   12-INCH PIZZA
         OR 10-INCH DEEP PIE

Prepare Filling and let stand while making pie crust.

In large mixing bowl, mix dry ingredients. Cut in butter until mixture resembles coarse crumbs. Add sour cream, stirring until dough forms into a ball. Press into 12-inch pizza pan. Bake at 375° for 12 to 15 minutes. Remove from oven.

Stir Filling and pour over crust. Sprinkle bacon evenly over Filling. Return to oven. Bake 25 to 30 minutes longer. Serve warm.

Filling: Mix in order given; blend well.

*For use with Pillsbury's Best Self-Rising Flour, omit soda and salt.

Tip: Pie may be baked in 10-inch pie pan at 375° for 30 to 35 minutes or until center is firm.

Bacon 'N Cheese Puff Pie
by Mrs. Richard Wurzburger, Scottsdale, Arizona

10 slices bacon, cut into 1-inch pieces
1 can Pillsbury Refrigerated Quick
   Crescent Dinner Rolls
2 medium tomatoes, sliced
½ teaspoon salt
   Pepper
5 slices American cheese
3 eggs, separated
¾ cup dairy sour cream
½ cup Pillsbury's Best All Purpose
   Flour*
½ teaspoon salt
   Paprika

OVEN 350°   9-INCH PIE

Fry bacon until crisp; drain. Unroll crescent dough and separate into 8 triangles. Place dough triangles in ungreased 9-inch pie pan, pressing together to form a crust. Sprinkle bacon over crust. Top with tomato slices; season with salt and pepper. Place cheese slices over top.

Beat egg whites until stiff. Set aside. In large mixing bowl, combine egg yolks, sour cream, flour, salt and a dash of pepper. Blend well. Gently fold beaten egg whites into mixture until a few lumps of egg white remain. Do not over blend. Pour mixture over cheese layer. Sprinkle with paprika. Bake at 350° for 35 to 40 minutes or until crust and top are golden brown and knife inserted in center comes out clean.

*For use with Pillsbury's Best Self-Rising Flour, omit salt.

Tips: Pie may be assembled and held uncovered in refrigerator up to 4 hours before baking.

For added flavor, substitute ½ teaspoon onion salt for salt in puff topping.

Bake Off Cook Book / 1968 / Fork 'N' Finger Onion Pie & Bacon 'N' Cheese Puff Pie / Pillsbury Company

Oyster Bay Bake
by Mrs. Catherine Young, West Palm Beach, Florida

18 Ritz crackers, crumbled
1 can (17 oz.) cream style corn
2 cans (8 oz. each) oysters, drained
1 can (10½ oz.) condensed cream of
   mushroom soup
¼ cup milk or evaporated milk
1 cup (4 oz.) ½-inch cubes mild
   Cheddar cheese

Topping

½ cup butter
1 cup Pillsbury's Best All Purpose or
   Self-Rising Flour
18 Ritz crackers, crumbled
   Dash of pepper

OVEN 450°   6 TO 8 SERVINGS

Crumble the crackers into a greased 8-inch square baking dish or a 2-quart shallow casserole. Spread corn over crackers. Arrange oysters over corn. Combine undiluted soup, milk and cheese; spoon over oysters. Sprinkle Topping over casserole. Bake at 450° for 10 minutes, then at 350° for 30 minutes.

Topping: Cut butter into flour until mixture resembles coarse crumbs. Stir in crumbled crackers and pepper.

Variations: 2 cans (4½ oz. each) shrimp, drained or 1 can (6½ oz.) tuna, drained or 2 cups cubed cooked ham may be substituted for the oysters.

Grilled Cheese Sandwich Pie
by Mr. Bruce Boyde, Wilmington, Delaware

1 egg
¾ cup Pillsbury's Best All Purpose
   Flour*
½ teaspoon salt
⅛ teaspoon pepper
1 cup milk
1 cup (4 oz.) shredded Muenster
   cheese

OVEN 425°   4 MAIN DISH SERVINGS
       OR 24 APPETIZER SERVINGS

In small mixing bowl, combine egg, flour, salt, pepper and half of milk. Using a rotary beater, beat until smooth. Add remaining milk; beat until well blended. Stir in one-half of the cheese. Pour into a well-greased 8-inch pie pan. Bake at 425° for 30 minutes. Sprinkle remaining cheese over top and bake just until cheese is melted, about 2 minutes.

*Self-Rising Flour is not recommended for use in this recipe.

Tip: Batter may be prepared ahead and refrigerated for an hour before baking.

Bake Off Cook Book / 1968 / Oyster Bay Bake & Grilled Cheese Sandwich Pie / Pillsbury Company

206

*Prize Winning Recipes / 1960 / American Beauty
Macaroni Company / Front and back cover*

*65 Prize Recipes From The South / 1935 / Why Dixie's finest cooks choose... /
Swift's Jewel Shortening / Swift & Company*

➤ Women's magazines have been a source for expert advice and new recipes since the advent of cheap printing in the late 1800s. *Good Housekeeping* Magazine since 1909 issued its 'Good Housekeeping Seal of Approval' to products that passed their testing regimen. In later years, the 'Seal' became an effective marketing tool and led to many partnerships between the magazine and advertisers. Its trustworthy reputation led many cooks to try some of their more, ahem, experimental recipes.

Egg and Cheese and Spaghetti and Rice Dishes / 1958 / Swiss Cheese Pie & Macaroni Inverness / Good Housekeeping Cookbooks

Creamy Spaghetti and Meat Balls

2 tablesp. butter or margarine
1 4-oz. can sliced mushrooms, drained
1 can spaghetti and meat balls in tomato sauce
⅓ cup sliced pitted ripe olives
⅓ cup commercial sour cream

In hot butter in saucepan, sauté mushrooms until heated. Add spaghetti and meat balls and olives; heat. Stir in sour cream; heat. Serve at once.

Makes 2 or 3 servings

Macaroni Bake

½ lb. macaroni, in 1½" pieces; or ½ lb. elbow macaroni (2 cups)
½ lb. grated process Cheddar cheese
9 tomato slices
1 tablesp. butter or margarine
¾ teasp. salt
¼ teasp. pepper
1 cup commercial sour cream

1. Start heating oven to 350°F. Cook macaroni as label directs; drain.

IN THE COLOR PHOTO ON PAGE 52
—Speedy Spanish Rice, page 62.

2. In 1½-qt. casserole, arrange one third of macaroni, then one third of cheese, then 3 tomato slices. Dot with one third of butter; sprinkle with one third of salt and pepper; then spread with one third of sour cream. Repeat until all ingredients are used, ending with sour cream.
3. Bake, covered, 30 min.

Makes 6 servings

Susan's Macaroni, Tomato, and Cheese
(Pictured on page 51)

2 cups macaroni, broken into 2½" pieces (½ lb.)
4 teasp. butter or margarine
¾ cup fresh bread crumbs
4 teasp. minced onions
2 tablesp. butter or margarine
1 tablesp. flour
¼ teasp. dry mustard
¾ teasp. salt
Speck pepper
2 cups milk
2 cups grated process Cheddar cheese (½ lb.)
2 medium tomatoes, in ½" slices (optional)

Start heating oven to 400°F. Cook macaroni as package directs; drain. In double boiler, melt 4 teasp. butter; toss with bread crumbs; set aside on waxed paper. In same double boiler, combine onion, 2 tablesp. butter, flour, mustard, salt, pepper; stir in milk; cook, stirring often, until smooth. Add 1½ cups of cheese; stir until melted. In 1½-qt. casserole, place half of macaroni, all but 2 or 3 tomato slices, then rest of macaroni. Pour on cheese sauce; sprinkle with rest of cheese and buttered crumbs; arrange rest of tomato slices on top. Bake 20 min.

Makes 4 to 6 servings

Egg and Cheese and Spaghetti and Rice Dishes / 1958 / Macaroni (pictured, Speedy Spanish Rice) / Good Housekeeping Cookbooks

BACON-AND-EGG-SALAD SANDWICHES

Bacon-and-Egg-Salad Sandwiches

5 diced Hard-Cooked Eggs, page 5
6 slices crumbled crisp bacon
½ teasp. salt
⅛ teasp. pepper
2 tablesp. mayonnaise
1 teasp. prepared mustard
1 teasp. minced onion
1 tablesp. vinegar
8 slices buttered whole-wheat or white bread

Combine eggs, bacon, salt, and pepper; stir in combined mayonnaise, mustard, onion, and vinegar. Use to fill 4 full-sized sandwiches.

Bunwiches

3 chopped Hard-Cooked Eggs, page 5
3 tablesp. chopped green pepper
1 tablesp. minced onion
Bit minced garlic
1 tablesp. chopped pimento
2 tablesp. butter, margarine, or salad oil
2 tablesp. chili sauce
⅛ teasp. salt
Speck pepper
2 tablesp. grated process Cheddar cheese
6 frankfurter rolls

Day before: Mix together eggs, green pepper, onion, garlic, pimento, butter, chili sauce, salt, pepper, and cheese. With fork, scoop out centers of frankfurter rolls; fill with egg mixture. Wrap each roll in foil or waxed paper. Refrigerate.
To serve: Heat in 400°F. oven 8 min.

Makes 6 servings

Pickled Eggs

Strain juice from pickled beets or sweet pickles; dilute with water if strong. Use to cover shelled, hard-cooked eggs, page 5. Refrigerate 1 to 2 days—no longer.

16

IN THE COLOR PHOTO ON PAGE 17—Eggs Divan, page 12.

Egg and Cheese and Spaghetti and Rice Dishes / 1958 / Eggs Divan / Good Housekeeping Cookbooks

AMERICAN ADVERTISING COOKBOOKS 209

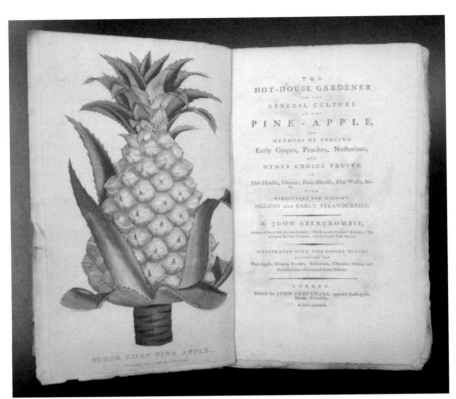

The Hot House Gardener by John Abercrombie / A primer
on how to raise pineapples in England. / 1789

Luxury Foods

As trade routes grew to cover the world, bananas and then pineapples acquired an exalted status of wealth and class. Bananas took over the Atlantic; pineapples dominated the Pacific region. Unlike temperamental banana clones which needed sandy, estuary-nourished soil, pineapples adapted and thrived in any hot climate regardless of soil composition. Early specimens were delivered to the royal courts of Spain and Portugal in the 1500s from their native growing region along the Parana and Paraguay rivers in South America. Pineapples were fragile to transport and often arrived rotted—which of course only added to their scarcity and value. European upper classes competed with each other to build elaborate 'pineries' or pineapple hothouses to cultivate the valuable fruit at home. During the two years of growth from planting until cultivation, these coddled pineapples required the services of a staff of servants to water, heat, and sun the plant. The final cost of a single fruit was the equivalent to a half-year's wage of the gardener who grew it.

Pineapples were valued by the elite to the extent that the image of the fruit was used to signify luxury and good taste. Its image adorned everything from delicate porcelain dishes, to wallpaper, to architectural finials, to ladies' hats. The symbol of the pineapple was the symbol of hospitality and a consummate host. The lady who would serve you pineapple at dinner was most fashionable and at the pinnacle of the aristocracy. Then as now, people sought to embody the tastes of the wealthy class without actually having the money or nepotistic blood alliances. Pineapples were so desirable that aspirational society ladies would rent them for dinner as the centerpiece of a bountiful display, but only to be admired, not eaten.

Fear of native foods from distant lands, excepting what was palatable to Europeans like bananas and pineapples, saw early Caribbean occupiers impose European agricultural methods and seed stock into the new and wholly incompatible geosystem. Crop experiments in wheat failed, so colonists looked to expand crops that they knew had value in European markets—bananas, pineapples, beef cattle, and sugar. Shipping fresh pineapples from Hispaniola to Madrid was prohibitively expensive. It outraged aristocratic sensibilities that 'peasants' in the colonies could enjoy these culinary delicacies while they could not.

This demand for the pineapple, much like that of the banana, inspired traders to take more risks—faster boats, attempts to chill cargos, anything to get the product to the people who wanted it. By the Victorian era, the rising middle classes, who had adopted the manners and pretenses of the upper classes, wanted the same taste of luxury. Social reformers took to writing anti-classist screeds decrying the pineapple as not the symbol of wealth and taste, but of economic stratification and moral weakness. This at a time when the poor of Whitechapel would line the docks waiting for merchant ships to pay a penny for a taste of the pineapples rejected by costermongers as too rotted.

Sugar solved this problem. Pineapple jams, sugared pineapple chips, and most commonly, pineapple syrup, were processed in newly built Caribbean canneries. Chemically, the sugar reduced the water activity in the fruit preparation which then inhibited bacterial growth, allowing, if not the pineapples themselves, at the very least their essence to be transported back to the clamoring masses in Europe.

King Sugar

Sugar cane is native to the Indian subcontinent and southeast Asia. Persian conquerors first encountered the grass circa 500 B.C. They exported then cultivated sugar cane, which grew into a valued commodity and helped establish the 'Silk Road' trading routes. Cooks and traders well knew the food-preserving properties of sugar and salt by the 1700s. Sugar's extraordinarily high value drove traders and governments to find more land where they could grow sugar as well as more people to do the labor.

Sugar cane plantations were established on various Caribbean islands by Spain with enslaved peoples in the early 1500s. Columbus' charter from the Spanish monarchy was not to 'discover a new world' but to establish new areas to grow sugar with free land and enslaved people. The wealth of the New World wasn't the fabled gold of the Aztecs, but that of land to be conquered and occupied.

The English soon followed the Spaniards to the Caribbean Islands and then further up the Atlantic coast in search of arable land to establish sugar plantations. This land grab by the Europeans resulted in a divvying up of the 'known' world into a system of European monarchies and their client colonies. During the two hundred or so years of exploration and colonization, war soon followed. The first true worldwide conflict commonly named the Seven Years' War began in 1756 and lasted until 1763. (It is more accurately referred to in Francophone Canada by as *La Guerre de la Conquete* or The War of Conquest.)

The various treaties enacted at the negotiated end of that war have consequences today. The current language and governmental structures of the modern world bear the marks of this colonial past. France traded a significant portion of Canada to England for the islands of Guadeloupe, St. Lucia, and Martinique. During the negotiations that concluded with the Treaty of Paris, the Dutch opted to keep their sugar-producing colonies of Suriname and St. Maarten instead of New Amsterdam (New York City). Spain retook possession of the Philippines and Cuba while gaining Florida from the French. England claimed hegemony over large swaths of Canada, Central America, and the Caribbean.

Indeed, this was the first worldwide war as battles for territory were fought on the African continent, the Indian subcontinent and along the southeast Asian trading strongholds. Though skirmishes cropped up in the ensuing years, the boundaries established by the Seven Years' War remained more or less intact until World War I. The relative diplomatic stability allowed for the European powers to pour their energies into developing their colonial states into economic generators. England mastered the circular route of enslaving people from their African colonies, transporting them to their Caribbean and American colonies as

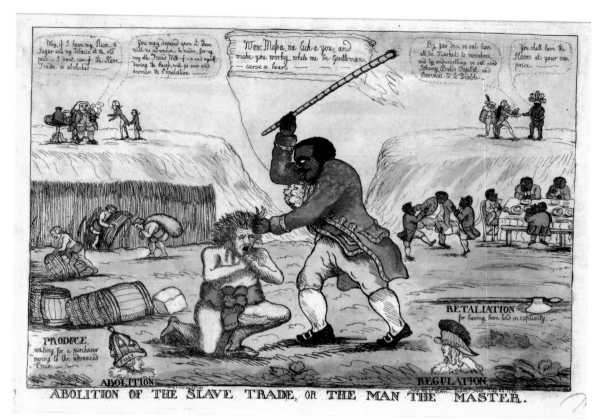

British pro-slavery cartoon / William Dent / 1789

labor, then exporting the goods back to Europe. Portugal enslaved the most people during the colonial period, but from the 1620s to the English abolition of slavery in 1833, historians estimate that the British transported 3.4 million people from Africa to the Americas to labor. Further analysis shows that of the total enslaved peoples, both captured and born enslaved, 55% worked on sugar plantations.

Spanish and Portuguese traders sailed an ovular South America to the South Asian 'Spice Islands' route, following trade winds and currents, for nearly two hundred years before English Captain James Cook decided to navigate through the middle of the oval on his mission to follow the path of the planet Venus. (This was a secret mission to discover the fabled land of Australia.) As he sailed the Pacific Ocean over the course of ten years, he explored and claimed for Britain many Pacific islands including those now known as Hawaii.

The northern Pacific Hawaiian islands proved to be both bountiful and strategic to the empire builders of Europe. English, French, and Spanish adventurers all ventured to 'assist' the existing royal family in modernizing the kingdom. Pineapples arrived on the islands in the early 1800s and grew to rival whaling and sugar as lucrative commodities. The remoteness of the Hawaiian Islands fostered a virtual détente as each European power upheld the Hawaiian monarchy while establishing individual ports and small plantations.

American Hegemony

The post-Revolutionary United States, freed from their British masters, was concerned about the other colonial powers that surrounded the young country. Revolution was in the air in the Americas as the South and Central American colonies were striving to break free of Spain and Portugal. After fighting and winning another war against the British in 1812–1814 put to rest the notion that the North American territories could be reconquered, the Americans decided that the best defense against incursion was to develop a strategy that prevented the Europeans from meddling in the Americas. Though smarting from the battle loss to the Americans, the British decisively won the Napoleonic wars which gave them the naval superiority in Europe to informally agree with the Americans—partnership would be the key to economic growth and a more tangible expression of power.

These new alliances fed the burgeoning American taste for empire as they laid claim to the Hawaiian territories as in their 'sphere of influence' as outlined in the Monroe Doctrine. The Americans added a new weapon to the conqueror's arsenal, one honed in her Puritanical roots; the Americans, unlike the Europeans, did not invade with guns but with God on their side.

The American Board of Commissioners for Foreign Missions, established in 1810 from an elite group of young Protestants, were the descendants of the founding Puritan families. They were inspired by the Great Awakening to preach throughout the Americas just as the English were doing in Africa and Asia. The first Congregationalist mission to the Hawaiian Islands arrived in 1820. As was the custom, these missionaries were often young married couples and were encouraged to build expatriate communities in the territories they occupied. Hawaii had an established European enclave which allowed these industrious missionaries to efficiently proselytize among the indigenous Hawaiians, spreading Western culture and destabilizing the tradition of communal subsistence farming, as well as the established monarchy. By the 1850s, these scions of the great Boston families encouraged more émigrés who established large-scale, colonial sugar plantations.

Daniel Dole came to Honolulu in 1841 with a large missionary group from Boston. The families, both newly arrived and long established, were interconnected by marriages and business alliances. Hawaii was still a sovereign nation, albeit one influenced by the sugar plantation owners and exporters. A skirmish between the Americans and British led to the British entirely taking control of the islands in 1843. The United States retaliated with exorbitant tariffs which left the Hawaiian government nearly bankrupted. After being reminded of the tenets of the Monroe Doctrine and some practical deal-making, the British returned governance of the Hawaiian Islands to the ruling Kamehameha Dynasty.

The American missionaries and plantation owners recognized an opportunity to seize power. They were the children of the original colonizers and identified themselves as Hawaiian. For a 20-year period beginning in the 1870s, the white Hawaiians sought and gained more control of the government and constitution. Opposition to a single issue fueled them: the royal policy, informed by their animistic religion, was that land could never be

214

sold, only leased. Through a series of collusive political maneuvers and cooperation of the United States Army, the white Hawaiians orchestrated a coup that left Queen Liliuokalani deposed and imprisoned by 1893. One of the main organizers of the coup was Queen Liliuokalani's chief advisor and Daniel Dole's son, Sanford Dole, aided by the fellow children and grandchildren of the missionaries. Dole and his group declared the Islands the Republic of Hawaii and himself installed as President. The new Republic of Hawaii quickly enacted a new constitution and created laws to allow for private ownership of land.

Queen Liliuokalani of Hawaii / 1887

President Dole wrote to his young cousin, James Dole, in 1899 about the business opportunities in the new republic. At 22, James took his savings (about $16,000) and left for Hawaii. His Harvard agricultural degree served him well as he quickly bought 64 acres in Oahu and began to plant pineapple. His operation proved wildly successful. Dole understood that pineapple's fragility prevented shipping the fresh fruit, and built canneries alongside his plantations. He soon realized that if operations expanded, he could corner the market, and the ability to grow, preserve, package, and ship pineapples directly to the United States ensured he controlled every aspect of the process.

The United States annexed the Hawaiian Islands in 1898. Sanford Dole stepped down as President but assumed the role of Governor until 1903 when he accepted the position of District Court judge. The extended Dole family in Hawaii was, of course, prominent in business and politics, but the original Boston branch of the family even more so. In 1922 when James Dole presented the extended family with his idea to form a real monopoly, all members agreed and invested. Cousin Sanford then helped to arrange the purchase of the Hawaiian island of Lanai. Dole and his Hawaiian Pineapple Company (the family thought it prudent to leave their name off the company door to hide the obvious nepotistic connections) quickly grew to provide 75% of the world's pineapple supply.

The Great Depression of the early 1930s saw Dole take a substantial financial loss as demand for the luxurious pineapple disappeared. Members of the network of the missionary families who invested in each others' companies, referred to as The Big Five, took control of the Hawaiian Pineapple Company. The Big Five have diversified into holding and investing companies; C & H Sugar, Castle & Cook, Dole, Amfac, Alexander & Baldwin are the original Big Five. Though most have been capitalized and sold, the descendants of the original Boston missionaries continue to reap their financial and spiritual rewards.

Sanford B. Dole / Counsel to the Hawaiian royal family, coup plotter, President of Hawaii, and District Court judge. / c.1890s

Workers harvesting pineapple / Hawaii / c. 1900s

Yanqui **Go South**

The countries of Central America, Honduras, Guatemala, Nicaragua, El Salvador, and Belize all share a founding year—1821. As the European colonial systems divvied up the world in the aftermath of the Seven Years' War, the regions formerly controlled by Spain and England declared themselves sovereign, no longer beholden to their European masters. However, as happened with most former colonies, the wealth had been stripped and exploited while the population was left impoverished by their former masters. The United States, as witnessed in Hawaii, told Old Europe that the Western Hemisphere, save for a few benevolent exceptions, was now theirs and to butt out.

These new countries had minimal infrastructure to create and collect revenues, which meant that plans for modernization required outsourcing. In their Year Zero, a feudal system of ruling families came to and remained in power with names that we still recognize—Somoza, Trujillo, Fanjul and more in a nearly unbroken line from then to today. The old chestnut describing modern American foreign policy in Central America ("He's a son of a bitch, but he's our son of a bitch") has been attributed to every United States President and purported to be about every Central American leader. Conditions that were so favorable to the unbridled 'capitalism' as practiced by the robber barons reliant on cheap and enslaved labor freely existed in the wilds of Central America.

216

The United States of the 1850s was a country in the throes of growing pains. The sheer size of the nation made it nearly ungovernable as individual states established laws contradictory to the Constitution and Federal law. These fights over 'State Rights' were fueled by a singular issue—slavery. The Southern states legally allowed for slavery and had built its entire economy on the practice. With the vile Dred Scott decision of 1857 that decreed that no formerly enslaved person could be a citizen of the United States and essentially nullified abolitionist laws in the Northern states, advocates of slavery saw an opportunity.

The Knights of the Golden Circle was a society devoted to pro-slavery U.S. expansion into Mexico, the Caribbean, and Central America. Founded in 1854, they saw the growing abolitionist movement as the wedge that would divide the country. In their worldview, it would be better to have two countries, with the Confederacy of States growing southward to establish new slaveholding territories. Our elementary school history would have us believe that the Mason-Dixon Line dividing Free States and Territories from slaveholding states was a clear demarcation. It was not. Ideas, both noble and virulent, are not separated by an arbitrary mark on a map. Many members and advocates of the Knights of the Golden Circle were Northerners whose businesses were dependent on the Southern slave economies. Others were racists, plain and simple. Though a small group, they held influence in commercial and military organizations.

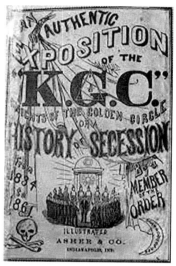

An Authentic Exposition of the Knights of the Golden Circle / Front cover / 1863

The United States government allowed and encouraged citizens to apply for charters that would establish new towns and developments in the unorganized western regions. Members of the Knights of the Golden Circle asked for charters in what is now Texas and New Mexico. Other members funded excursions to Central America knowing that they had tacit support from President James Buchanan. In 1859, Senator Sam Houston introduced a (failed) bill to Congress that would establish a United States protectorate over Mexico, Nicaragua, Costa Rica, Guatemala, Honduras, and San Salvador (El Salvador). By the time the Civil War broke out in 1861, embedded in the American political thinking was the notion that the land south of the Rio Grande River to the South American continent belonged to the United States.

What is a *banana?*

Modern bananas are a hybrid berry of the *Musa* family of bushes native to equatorial African and Pacific regions. Kin to plantains, the first bananas were brought to the Caribbean islands by Portuguese Jesuits in the early 1500s to feed the newly enslaved Carib people and kidnapped West Africans. These 'bananas' were high in complex carbohydrates and less sweet than their modern version. African and Pacific cuisines ate them like cassavas and yams—a filling starch base for meats and vegetables.

Botanical illustration of banana /
Pierre-Joseph Redouté / c. 1820s

Bananas thrive in tropical equatorial climates with a sandy nutri-ent-dense soil. They are unique as an agriculture crop because they're asexual reproducers. Each banana you eat is a clone from the ur-banana grown in the plantations in Central America. The ear-liest known depiction of cultivated bananas is in cave paintings in Malaysia. The process as shown in those old drawings, though now mechanized, is substantially the same as a thousand years ago: take a cutting of the tuber-like root, plant it into the ground, and wait.

As a wild plant, bananas competed for territory and nutrients in an environment with thousands of other flora. Its system of growth by sending out rooted tentacles and forcing itself out of the earth as a slow-growing clone was harmless in a diverse ecosystem. As a cultivated plant, the banana's reproduction method has left it wholly vulnerable to diseases. Spores and microbes, which are continually evolving their DNA to become efficient predators, have an easy tar-get in the banana, which is a cloned, evolutionary dud which has not and cannot develop a natural defense against microbial invasion.

Sigatoka is a spore-based disease that blows in on the wind and attacks the leaves caus-ing them to die, which exposes the undeveloped fruit to the sun and premature ripening, killing it before harvest. Panama Disease is a microbial root disease that infects the cells and chokes off the stem system, robbing the plant of water. Sigatoka and Panama Disease have evolved into increasingly active killers that are now present in every banana plan-tation on earth. There is no fungicide, pesticide, or chemical killer that can defeat these diseases, though commercial growers have experimented with a wide range of poisons that have wreaked havoc on the Central American landscape. The banana you eat today is the third cultivated variant in the modern era. The 'Cavendish' in supermarkets today is the banana of the post-1950s. It replaced the 'Big Mike' which was a replacement for the 'Red Macabau' and 'Lady Finger' of the late 1800s.

The eunuch banana combined with industrial monoculture agriculture means that these virulent diseases decimate more than a wild enclave of plants, but the entire worldwide sup-ply of banana plants. For companies reliant on banana-based revenue, the prospect of losing the cultivated acres to human rights advocates wanting fair wages and a clean environment or the fruit itself to disease is an existential threat. Business leaders and investors employed a 'by-any-means-necessary' strategy to protect their plantations from social and political unrest, while scientists for Chiquita Banana and Dole Foods are racing against the clock to discover and develop a new variety because this is it—bananas are on a path to extinction.

Food science is working to give bananas the DNA evolution that nature omitted. Research includes changing and adding genetic elements to make bananas disease-re-sistant while maintaining the characteristics familiar to consumers. The growers contend that genetic modification will solve the threat of extinction and negate the need for pes-ticides. Even so, there are hundreds of years of cleanup and land reclamation needed to restore the Central American landscape. The restitution owed to the people of Honduras, Guatemala, and Costa Rica has not yet been addressed by banana-growing corporations.

Banana merchant in Detroit, Michigan / 1902

Railroad and Banana Invasion

Unlike the semi-benevolent takeover of Hawaii, the transformation of Honduras, Guatemala, Costa Rica, and El Salvador was led by the Boston businessmen who *weren't* Christian missionaries. The rarefied world of the Boston elite made little room for outsiders, even rich ones. Andrew Preston was as wealthy as the extended Dole family but not considered their social equal. He was a fruit importer who bought and transported produce from the Caribbean, which included, but was not exclusively, bananas. Business was good, but exploded after the 1876 Centennial Exhibition kicked off the banana frenzy. Preston had the foresight and acumen to expand his operations and purchased banana plantations in Jamaica. He was the first to embrace the idea of controlling every aspect of the growing, harvesting, shipping, selling process. He partnered with ship owner and captain Lorenzo Baker to form the Boston Fruit Company.

Demand for bananas increased as the fruit moved from luxury item to commodity. Preston's Boston Fruit Company made improvements to the quality of bananas grown on his plantations. He selected trees based on quantity and size of the fruit, and he changed the varietal, planting the bigger, yellow-colored 'Big Mike' instead of the smaller red-colored 'Red Macau.' He sought out new technologies to help him gain market share, and because he owned the production, transportation, and distribution, he could undercut every other grower and importer on price which allowed him to dominate the market.

Map of Central America / c. 1840s

The other grand technological advances displayed at the Centennial Exhibition created opportunities for businessmen of all stripes. The development of the steam train meant that railroads were a must-have for economic growth in every country. Whatever wasn't owned by the hearty Scots of eastern Pennsylvania like Carnegie was owned by the New Yorkers who invested in growing rail systems competing to crisscross the States.

The Knights of the Golden Circle and their comrades were not the only people interested in Central America. Until the opening of the Panama Canal in 1914 and the development of the transcontinental rail lines throughout the 1870s–1900s, shipping produce and raw materials from the east coast to the west meant sailing around the Tierra del Fuego at the tip of South America. New York shipping baron Cornelius Vanderbilt held a monopoly on those commercial shipping routes. As the western expansion opened up more territory to trade, Vanderbilt realized the potential in rail and founded, sold, and sat on the board of directors for many of the small railway companies popping up in the United States. To Vanderbilt, rail was but a component of a shipping modality; his most pressing concern was shortening the cross-country sea voyage.

The dream of breaking through the narrow isthmus that joins Central to South America was first conceived by the Holy Roman Emperor Charles V in 1534, who sought a faster route from Spain to Peru while avoiding the Portuguese in Brazil. Breaking through the Panamanian isthmus animated each ruling powerbroker from the King of Scotland to Thomas

Jefferson. It was the engineering Holy Grail, with many fools and geniuses proposing ideas, but no genuine attempt began until the late 1800s after the successful completion of the American Erie Canal and later the French triumph at Suez. It was the French that won the contract to begin the Panama project in 1881.

The Panamanian isthmus was the shortest route in actual mileage, yet there were other routes considered through the Mexican Tehuantepec isthmus, Costa Rica, and across Nicaragua. As engineers debated feasibility and countries argued for control of the proposed canal, Cornelius Vanderbilt advocated for the rival Nicaraguan canal design. With no time to dither about feasibility studies, Vanderbilt implemented his personal solution—an expansion of his Accessory Transit Company which would use steamships to carry cargo up the San Juan River from the Pacific Ocean to Lake Nicaragua, then transfer goods to rail for the last hundred miles to waiting Vanderbilt ships at the Pacific port of Punta Brito. Vanderbilt's innovation and speed nearly halved the cost of shipping goods transnationally.

In 1855 Knights of the Golden Circle member William Walker established a new American colony of mercenaries on the small strip of land between the Pacific Ocean and Lake Nicaragua near the city of Rivas, where Vanderbilt-owned ships transferred goods to Vanderbilt-owned horse carts that were carried overland to Vanderbilt-owned ships on their final journey to San Francisco. He received charters from the United States government to establish colonies along the Pacific coast of Mexico, but they failed. Walker went further south at the nominal invitation of a rival Nicaraguan general in the midst of mounting a coup against the ruling Somoza family, but soon established himself as ruler of Nicaragua with the blessing of United States President Franklin Pierce.

Though Walker subdued the rival Nicaraguan generals, in an act of hubris he took on a power higher than any government—Cornelius Vanderbilt. Walker was quickly defeated over the course of a few months after Vanderbilt persuaded the bordering Costa Rican government to defend against Walker's incursions. Walker's defeated mercenaries fled to New Orleans as Walker was arrested and given over to the United States Navy. He was never tried (many suspected that this was due to the support of President Pierce) but was sent to British Honduras at the behest of English colonists looking to establish an independent region. The Hondurans, still fighting border skirmishes, had no use for Walker and separatists; he was arrested and executed by a Honduran firing squad in September 1860.

Walker's defeat was more than a military one—Vanderbilt, and the Northern captains of industry envisioned a future of global commerce without slavery. Yes, they had derived benefits from a slave-based economy, but the Industrial Revolution changed the nature of work as modern labor required skills that enslaved people had no opportunity to learn. The abolitionist capitalist's stance was based on financial ideals, not moral ones; industrialists had done the calculations and found that enslaved workers are less productive, more volatile, and at the bottom line, more expensive. The Knights of the Golden Circle's mission to develop pro-slavery colonies in Central America died with Walker. But the model of proxy warfare on behalf of United States business entities was replicated again and again throughout Central America. The lesson learned by Americans striving for expansion and influence in Central America was that covert instead of overt maneuvers yielded the best results.

Stock Certificate from Meiggs Wharf Company / 1874

Yes, We Have No *Bananas*

New Yorker Henry Meiggs came west to California with the Gold Rush in the 1840s to begin in the lumber trade but soon moved to San Francisco to invest in property development. A series of bad deals left Meiggs broke. There is debate as to whether he embezzled or defrauded the city of San Francisco's street-building fund through an investment scheme—he wasn't indicted, but he and five million dollars sailed into Santiago, Chile to begin his next career: railroad building. Called 'Don Enrique' by the Peruvians, he built his fame and fortune constructing the rail system built in Chile and Peru. He was a de facto dictator of Peru for nearly 20 years as he used his position with the railroad to control which exports went to European countries at what price. His corrupt dealings left Chile and Peru nearly bankrupted upon his death.

Before his demise in 1877, the ruling oligarch Montealegre family of Costa Rica contacted Meiggs to build them a railroad. Costa Rica had access to the Pacific, but its most lucrative commodity, coffee, had to travel around Cape Horn and on an extended journey around the Southern Hemisphere to reach the growing markets in the eastern United States. The United States and Cornelius Vanderbilt were already proposing cutting a canal through Central America, ideally along the San Juan River that divided Costa Rica from Nicaragua, but President (and former coup leader) General Tomás Guardia Gutiérrez could not wait. He signed a contract for a railroad to be built from the high plateau capital of San José to the swampy Atlantic region of Limón. Meiggs signed the deal with the intent of handing the project to his sister's sons, Minor and Henry Keith. Henry was with his Uncle Meiggs as they signed the contract, little knowing of or understanding that the terrain in Costa Rica was nothing like Peru or Chile.

Limón Province is today much as it was in the 1870s: a forested mangrove swamp. The goal of the Keith brothers was to begin at opposite ends of the proposed rail line and meet in the middle. The elder brother, Henry, started in the city of San José located on a mesa in the central highlands. Younger brother Minor, recruited to work on the project after a series of failed business ventures, was to begin in Limón, the small Atlantic port city, and make his way westward.

To say that Minor Keith got the worst end of the project is an understatement. Limón Province was sparsely populated with native Carib enclaves and small settlements of mestizo subsistence fishermen. Without workers on site, Minor's first job was to recruit able bodies. In post-Civil War New Orleans, he found displaced soldiers and mercenaries rousted from William Walker's Nicaraguan 'kingdom' ready to take on new challenges. The Keith brothers and Uncle Meiggs woefully underestimated the hostility of the terrain. Imported American works balked at the harsh conditions, then soon fell victim to tropical diseases. Minor next recruited workers from Italy, but they too succumbed to rampant malaria, yellow and dengue fevers.

By 1880, Minor Keith laid 25 miles of track and lost his three brothers in the Costa Rican Rail venture to tropical diseases. It wasn't until he recruited African-Jamaican workers that they made progress measured in feet, not miles. The financially troubled Costa Rican government defaulted on payments to Keith, so he brokered a deal to take land instead of cash, leaving Keith owning close to one million acres of areas adjacent to his rail lines. He also married into the Costa Rican oligarchy which made him related to the President and nearly all the Cabinet members during various times of his life.

While Keith was attempting to build his railway, French engineer Ferdinand du Lesseps was in the midst of the first attempt at constructing the Panama Canal. French workers defecting from du Lesseps' project came to work for the Costa Rican Railway bringing a favorite local food item with them—Gros Michel ("Big Mike") bananas and the rootstock to grow more. Keith began experimenting with planting root clones along the cleared acres along the railways. The bananas proved much more adaptable to the terrain than the railroad.

There were other small banana growers throughout the Caribbean and Central American regions who sold their stocks to fruit importers who marketed bananas as an exotic luxury. The Centennial Exhibition in 1876 had brought bananas to a nationwide audience and began both the craze and frenzied demand for bananas. Keith took advantage of his supply ships bringing construction materials from New Orleans and sent the formerly empty boats back loaded with bananas. The Costa Rican railroad was completed in 1890 but continued to lose money. Keith funded the losses with his expanding banana business. He acquired more plantation land in Colombia and became the largest supplier of bananas in the region. In 1899, he needed a cash infusion to fuel further growth and merged with Andrew Preston's Boston Fruit Company to form the United Fruit Company. And United Fruit Company changed how we eat, how we advertise, and how we fight wars.

Banana harvest in Guatemala / 1928

United Fruit **Takes Over the World**

United Fruit has been scattered throughout this book. It is when Bernays and United Fruit join forces that we reach the pinnacle of how corporations influenced how and what we eat and why food production is a geopolitical and environmental issue to be reckoned with.

Sam Zemurray wasn't a Boston Brahmin or one of the four hundred families of New York. Born to a Jewish family in what is now Moldova, Shmuel Zmurri immigrated to the United States with his aunt in 1891. They arrived in Selma, Alabama to join her husband (his uncle) in the family grocery business. It was there that young Sam first encountered bananas. Encouraged by his family, he took his uncle's stake money to try his hand at fruit trading at the port of New Orleans, where all the Caribbean growers sent their produce. He made a tactical error (or a brilliant move, depending on which version of the story you want to believe) of purchasing ripe bananas.

Bananas in the 1890s were cut and shipped while green to maximize their viability and get them to stores before they rotted. A ripe banana in New Orleans resulted in a rotten banana in New York City. Most growers threw out the 'ripes' dockside, as the fruit buyers from the East wouldn't take them. Zemurray bought the 'ripes,' then quickly resold them for a nominal profit to small grocers throughout the Gulf Coast region. Within three years he was Sam the Banana Man, notorious on the New Orleans docks with his six-foot height and Eastern European-accented English and Spanish.

In a few years, he saved enough money to purchase a small steamer and a plot of land in Honduras to grow his own bananas. United Fruit owned most of Costa Rica, but Honduras presented opportunities to rival banana men. The country was bankrupted and in debt to the J.P.

Morgan Company. Honduras owed so much money that Morgan Bank asked Secretary of State Philander Chase Knox to help them collect the debt by making Honduras raise and collect more taxes. Knox encouraged the ousting of their president, Manuel Bonilla, and installed someone friendlier to servicing the Morgan Bank debt. Zemurray too owed the Morgans money when he borrowed millions of dollars for his land speculations in Honduras. Zemurray appealed to Secretary Knox for leniency with the Morgans but was told in no uncertain terms: no.

Lee Christmas (on white horse) / Honduras / 1900

Zemurray headed back to his home in New Orleans only to discover deposed Honduran President Bonilla kicking his heels in the French Quarter. Zemurray offered to help get the president back into power. At the exact turn of the New Year 1912, a banana boat filled with mercenaries, guns, and Bonilla landed and quickly captured the island of Roatán and were on their way. Leading the troops was the most celebrated mercenary of the day, Lee Christmas. A former Louisiana railway worker, Christmas was feared and respected for his instinctive war-fighting strategies. As much myth as a man (he was rumored to eat glass), his prowess in winning asymmetrical battles earned his reputation. The coup was won at La Ceiba, and Bonilla was installed as President once more. Zemurray was rumored to use the threat of a Christmas-led coup as negotiating leverage with other governments who asked for either too much in taxes or kickbacks.

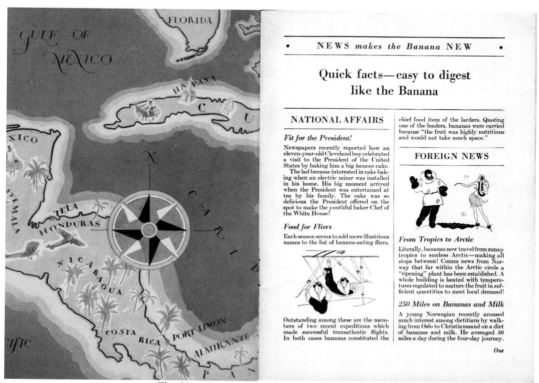

The New Banana / United Fruit / In addition to nutrition, use, and recipes, the 'News' page painted a rosy picture of 'Bananaland.' / 1931

Zemurray's investment paid off. The new Bonilla-led government reduced his tax bill and granted Zemurray concessions on millions of acres of Honduran land. His business, named Cuyamel Fruit after his first plantation, continued to grow. In the ongoing battle for control of Central America, bananas won.

Andrew Preston died in 1924, secure in the knowledge that he led United Fruit to success. Preston introduced large refrigerated ships that could haul produce faster and farther. He spurred new research into banana monoculture and pesticides when the first fungal diseases appeared in 1903. He grew shareholder value while keeping costs low and suppressing worker uprisings. He was, at his death, a model of the American businessman.

Minor Keith, now in his 80s, felt Preston's death keenly. Though United Fruit was one company, the railway portion of the business was organized as a separate entity. In 1928,

Brothers, John Foster (r) and Allen Welsh (l) Dulles / 1948

he began the legal proceedings for United Fruit to absorb full ownership of the Costa Rican railways. Keith knew that the government of Costa Rica would fight against this merger as a foreign company owning their major rail lines was a matter of national security. There was too much at stake for United Fruit to lose this fight. In Minor Keith's last business corporate maneuver, he called his most trusted legal counsel, who happened to be a former Secretary of State and fellow New Yorker, Robert Lansing. Lansing recommended his nephews as lead attorneys.

Keith was familiar with the nephew's work. Under Lansing's tutelage, they argued to President Woodrow Wilson the case for a military dictatorship in Costa Rica. They lost that case but made an impression on Keith. The young Dulles brothers, John Foster and Allen, were perfect for the job. They successfully negotiated the merging of the Costa Rican railways into the official holdings of United Fruit in early 1929. Minor Keith died in June of 1929 having outlived the first generation of freebooters and banana men in Central America.

Minor Keith and Sam Zemurray were friends. The older man mentored the young man as they built their empires. Upon Keith's death, Zemurray looked back on his life. He was 53 and more prosperous than Croesus. He was a conscientious modern American Jew and felt that the anti-Semitism he escaped in pogrom-ridden Eastern Europe was spreading to the West. He was an active donor to Jewish community groups and an early supporter of Chaim Weitzmann's Zionist movement. He decided to retire from business to focus on his family and philanthropy.

United Fruit as managed by a board of directors did not share Minor Keith's affection for Zemurray and his competing banana business. The board consulted with the Dulles Brothers and other friends at the State Department to suss out antagonism to the idea of United Fruit buying Zemurray's Cuyamel Fruit Company. The State Department encouraged the transaction, feeling United Fruit's expanded presence would bring stability to Central America. The United States Government agreed to smooth the way for the deal. In 1930, over a few shared beers, Sam Zemurray sold out to United Fruit for cash and shares in the newly expanded company.

The Boston-based board of directors did not have the hands-on experience of their company's founders. They were investors and managers without a drop of adventuresome or mercenary blood in them. Within two years, United Fruit was crippled by debt and a plunging stock price. Zemurray lamented the demise of not only his company but of the legacy of his friend Minor Keith. His wealth was tied up in those stocks, and he was furious. He sent suggestions for improvement to the board only to be ignored. In 1933 he finally had enough. He bought up shares at prices driven low by the Depression until he held a controlling majority, then hied himself up to Boston for a board meeting. After listening to reports and discussions—none of which addressed the real financial concerns of United Fruit—he leaped up and in his heavy Eastern European accent shouted, "You gentlemen have fucked this company long enough." Sam the Banana Man was back, this time in charge of United Fruit.

Sam Zemurray / c. 1940s

United Fruit, **Take Two**

Zemurray recommitted himself to the success of United Fruit. The founding Puritanical Bostonians shunned media and subscribed to the beliefs of the previous generation of merchants: let the product speak for itself. Zemurray dismissed this antiquated notion and embraced the new field of public relations and every new style of advertising that came along. Before Preston and Keith's deaths, United Fruit set up an education department based on the Boston Cooking schools' model of scientific information presented in a calm and dignified manner. Zemurray took 'education' to new levels.

His initial instinct was to let journalists, who were making waves with muckraking stories exposing malfeasance in the food processing world, take a tour of the United Fruit plantations and operations. In his mind, everything was great. His plan backfired spectacularly. The junket left New Orleans on a banana boat to visit plantations in Guatemala and Honduras. Where United Fruit saw efficient operations, reporters saw oppressed workers of color in substandard housing, corrupt government officials, and management and executives living in luxurious gated communities. Journalists dubbed United Fruit 'El Pulpo,' or "the octopus," as it had tentacles in the political, social, economic, and cultural institutions throughout Central America.

Great White Fleet advertisement / 1942 / United Fruit / United Fruit turned their tourist fleet over to the United States war effort—and made sure to let consumers know the details of their contribution.

The United States was in the throes of the Great Depression, and for the first time throughout all the Americas, socialist and communist ideologies were viable as real political solutions for the working classes. American businesses, including United Fruit, were having none of it. The United States military became active in suppressing coups and controlling borders in the interest of the corporations and their shareholders. There's a reason the Marine Corps Hymn begins with the words 'From the Halls of Montezuma....' General Smedley Butler, who served 33 years with the Marines in Central America, summed up his career in his 1935 book *War Is A Racket*: "For the benefit of Wall Street, I helped in the rape of half a dozen Central American republics." The term 'Banana Republic' entered the Oxford English dictionary in 1935.

Zemurray and United Fruit escaped any indictments from the Roosevelt administration for their ruthless business practices even though testimony and evidence were presented to Congress. Taking non-indictment as an endorsement, Zemurray still had a public relations nightmare to contend with. Upon the recommendation of his crackerjack attorneys, John Foster and Allan Dulles, he hired their old comrade from the Center for Public Information, Edward Bernays. He was given carte blanche by Zemurray to remake the image of United Fruit and make bananas the favorite food of the nation.

Using his tried and true template, Bernays began his multifaceted approach to change the perception of bananas and United Fruit. Bernays took control of the 'education department' and hired an army of home economists to develop recipes using bananas in every conceivable manner. He published cookbooks containing both recipes and information about the exotic yet very American countries where bananas grow. He had United Fruit build a vacation resort on an older and now unused plantation site and sold holiday vacations to 'Bananaland,' a magical place much like the mythical "Fantasy Island" where dreams are made real.

Advertisement for United Fruit 'banana boat' tour to Jamaica / c. 1910s

Bernays also set up the nonprofit Middle America Information Bureau that produced glossy weekly reports to journalists about the beauty and bounty of not Central America, but Middle America. He tapped a friend from the Center for Public Information to manage the 'Latin America Report' geared toward businessmen and investors. He set to work with researchers to scour medical and scientific studies that showed bananas in a favorable light, and when they could find no more, United Fruit began funding scientists to explore the health benefits of bananas.

Bernays took Zemurray's real passion for philanthropy and made sure that every good deed was publicized. He encouraged Zemurray to fund schools in Honduras and fund

Chiquita Banana drawn by Dik Browne / 1944

research chairs at major American universities. United Fruit financed children's hospitals and clinics until the name brought to mind benevolence as well as bananas. As World War II emerged, United Fruit lent their banana boats to the government for troop and supply transport. These public-private partnerships were staffed with people chosen by Bernays and his friends, and the United Fruit legal advisors, the Dulles Brothers. They put in place people who would be loyal to United Fruit, the United States, and the Center for Public Information, which later came to be known as the Central Intelligence Agency.

Bernays had won the minds of Americans, but he needed to win the hearts too. Miss Chiquita Banana was born from the pen of cartoonist/illustrator Dik Browne in 1944. (Browne also drew the daily cartoon strips *Hagar the Horrible and Hi & Lois*.) The fruit-laden hat and sarong-wearing, singing and dancing banana made her first appearance in United Fruit cookbooks. She was a hit. United Fruit spent a significant amount of its advertising budget sponsoring national and local radio programs, Chiquita Banana was always a featured guest, singing with everyone from Bert Lahr (the Cowardly Lion from *The Wizard of Oz*) to Edgar Bergen and Charlie McCarthy (famed ventriloquist and his 'dummy'). Voiced by uncredited actresses and singers for years, she was made whole in the form of Carmen Miranda. Brazilian Carmen Miranda never claimed to be Chiquita, and United Fruit never claimed Miranda was Chiquita, but audiences made a connection for themselves that their favorite singing, dancing, sarong- and fruit-hat-wearing banana had come to life.

In the ten years from the coining of the phrase 'Banana Republic' to the end of World War II in 1945, United Fruit through the machinations of Edward Bernays morphed from a detested monopoly to a beloved supplier of the country's favorite fruit.

Gloriosa Victoria by Diego Rivera / 1954

El Pulpo

Sam Zemurray was personally devastated when the scope of the genocidal destruction of European Jewry by European fascists came to light. His earlier relationship with Chaim Weitzmann was revived, and his focus turned away from United Fruit to the Zionist cause of a Jewish homeland in Palestine. He funded the exodus of nearly 40,000 Jews from Europe to the Middle East. From 1945 to 1948, he used his British-registered banana boats to ferry weapons to Zionists fighting against the British army which occupied the Levant. He was a juxtaposition of ruthlessness and compassion that revealed itself when his passion was ignited. Zemurray was directly responsible for the overthrow of at least two governments on two continents. He finally retired as president of United Fruit in 1951.

Before his retirement, he wanted to ensure that the company would not fall into benign neglect from docile Boston-based investors as happened in 1930. There were four Cabot family members on the board of directors and he hand-picked Thomas Cabot as his successor. The Cabots were a Boston Brahmin family descended from the original Massachusetts Bay Colony settlers. Unlike many of the other Boston investor class, the Cabots had a taste for intrigue. They moved in and out of government with ease during the 1930s through the 1970s in every imaginable post from Ambassador to Secretary of State. The

Cabots were familiar with the Dulles brothers' work, not only for the Company but in clandestine government service.

Thomas served as president for one year before handing the reins over to his cousin Henry Cabot Lodge, who was later a Senator of Massachusetts and ran for President of the United States in 1960. Suffice to say, the Cabots were well-connected and well acquainted with the political and economic concerns of running United Fruit.

During World War II, the Dulles brothers resigned as counsel to United Fruit to take up positions in government. John Foster was a foreign policy advisor to Roosevelt rival Thomas Dewey, and then later appointed to fill a vacant New York State Senate seat. Allan moved directly to the Office of Strategic Services and served as a spymaster in Europe during the entirety of the war. As lifelong Republicans, they remained on governmental sidelines during the Democratic Truman administration but were tapped by incoming President Eisenhower to head up two essential cabinet positions in 1950. John Foster became Secretary of State, and Allan became the head of the newly reorganized Central Intelligence Agency.

World War II tamped down, but never eliminated socialist and communist sentiments in the Americas. In fact, a growing union movement and the positive results of Roosevelt's socialist-lite New Deal programs made people see the potential of a social-democratic political system. Corporations and Wall Street took the opposite view. Now that fascism had been defeated, the next enemy was socialism and communism as embodied by Russia and China. Priority one for the United States was that no communist-style government establish itself on the Western Hemisphere. Which countries were most likely to throw off the shackles of foreign debt, foreign ownership, and corrupt governments? The banana republics of Central America.

Guatemala elected a professed socialist, Colonel Jacobo Arbenz, in 1951. He campaigned on a land reform platform to nationalize the banana plantations and redistribute land to citizens. United Fruit, the owner of the majority of said plantations, was outraged. Private corporations bore the brunt of the financial losses when socialist and communist revolutions nationalized their operations. The Cabots were not about to let that happen in Central America. Edward Bernays was put to work.

Bernays created a barrage of press stories aimed at both the American public and elected officials. United Fruit supported the anti-communist hearings held by Senator Joseph McCarthy while whipping up fear of the horrors of communism to the general public. It sent weekly updates to Congress of ever-increasing outrages allegedly committed by Guatemalan president Arbenz. He organized journalist 'fact-finding' tours of peace-loving Colombia, then to the tension-filled unrest on the Guatemala plantations.

(All workers were instructed on how to answer reporters' questions.) Magazines and newspapers were happy to run the 'communist threat in Guatemala' stories as United Fruit lavished them with advertising dollars.

Eisenhower's Domino Theory informs United States foreign policy to this day: if one country becomes socialist/communist, then their neighbors will follow. By 1954, United Fruit had garnered enough public support. It was time to bring the team together. United Fruit majority shareholder and Ambassador to the United Nations Henry Cabot Lodge called President Eisenhower to make his case for a regime change in Guatemala. Eisenhower consulted his Secretary of State, John Foster Dulles, and received a briefing from CIA chief Allan Dulles—both confirmed, Guatemala was trouble, and if the Arbenz government remained in power it would be the first domino that would set off all the others.

In March of 1954, United Fruit treated journalists to unlimited food and drinks at a plantation on the Honduran border. A CIA-led band of U.S. commandos and mercenaries moved to remove President Arbenz from power. CIA agent and mission leader Howard Hunt had only one regret about the outcome of Operation Success—he had captured Arbenz defender Che Guevara, but let him go in a gentlemen's agreement that he leave the country. Guevara promptly left for Cuba.

Lessons Learned

"The United Fruit Co. in Guatemala, Or, Watch Out for the Top Banana" by Warren Sloat, AVILA (Avoid Vietnam in Latin America) / Pamphlet / c. 1960s.

United Fruit was pleased with the outcome in Guatemala but had caused too much ruckus in the national and international media. Reporters realized they had been rum-drinked into believing the 1954 coup story as spoonfed by Bernays. The United States Congress felt that McCarthy, United Fruit, and the CIA had gone too far. The Congress threatened an investigation into banana price-fixing. The more sedate of the Boston board members took control and in 1959 let Edward Bernays go. They had Chiquita Banana and the template built by Bernays; they didn't need him anymore.

United Fruit faced new challenges. The 1960s civil rights movement was a worldwide phenomenon as students, workers, and the poor gave voice to their collective grievances, and in Central America, United Fruit was the sui generis of most of the turmoil. The 1969 Football War between El Salvador and Honduras disrupted the banana trade and was the final straw for the struggling company. An ambitious investment banker from Lehman Brothers, Eli Black, using a newly acquired company began buying United Fruit Stock. Much like Sam Zemurry did in the 1930s, Eli Black went up to Boston to talk to the Board.

232

Eli Black was, like Zemurry, a proud and studious Jew. Born in Poland and descended from generations of rabbis, he viewed his work in banking as rescuing businesses from the brink of ruin and building wealth for his shareholders as a service to his community and country. The United Fruit board members heard Black's pitch and agreed to be acquired in 1970. Black assumed leadership of the newly named company, United Brands. He ran the company from his New York City office dealing with a succession of catastrophes.

In a PR move reminiscent of the glory days of Bernays, Black led United Brands-funded rescue and relief work in Nicaragua after the cataclysmic earthquake that decimated the capital city of Managua in 1972. Films of the relief work and subsequent rebuilding of the town gave hope that the new company was shifting its focus, as Black proclaimed, to partnerships with growers and the Central American countries. But the good feelings didn't last very long.

The bananas themselves were failing. The Sigatoka black fungus reached the Central American plantations in 1973 and quickly decimating the fruit. The OPEC-led oil crisis of the same year drove fuel prices up and was the harbinger of an economic recession. Culturally, millions of readers were turning on to Gabriel García Márquez's recently translated novel *One Hundred Years of Solitude*, whose plot was predicated on United Fruit's history in Central America, and shone a new light on the dark history of the fruit. Hurricane Fifi hit Honduras in September of 1974 and wiped out 90% of the plantations on the Atlantic side of the country. As United Brands desperately tried to save the banana and their company, advertising how to eat one is no longer a concern.

United Brands and Eli Black were near the breaking point. The Somoza family in Nicaragua worked with their old friends in the CIA to build a bulwark against the growing socialist worker movements embraced by citizens and condoned by the Catholic Church. The United States needed strength in the area and the company, who once controlled mercenaries and national armies, no longer had it. Guatemala filed legal injunctions and the United States government began investigating the stock sales that enabled the purchase of the company. Indictments were rumored to be coming, and the stock price tanked. On the cold morning of February 3, 1975, Eli Black smashed open the massive window in his Park Avenue office with his briefcase. After throwing the briefcase out the cragged opening, he crawled onto the ledge and jumped.

United Brands skulked into its corner and lay dormant as a diversified holding company. The election of Jimmy Carter in 1976 and his promise of a New Deal for Central America stifled the overt reactionary juntas in the banana-growing countries for a few years. But the election of Ronald Reagan four years later signaled a throwback to 1950s-era anti-communism and free rein for the American-funded and led anti-worker movements. Free-trade agreements and relaxed laws found bananas once again a lucrative commodity. In the early 1990s the banana business was spun off and sold to a Swiss financial holding company who finally broke with the old name of United Fruit and embraced the lovable mascot as their company name; they are now known as Chiquita Banana.

Sugar Information, Inc. advertisement / 1966

Changes in the
Food Landscape

The 1950s through the 1970s were the pinnacle of advertising cookbooks. The era was the culmination of everything America thought it should be as envisioned by the founding Puritans. The image portrayed back to us was of that clean, Christian, nuclear family. The reality was of course much different. The idealized American family never did reflect reality. The United States has long been at war with itself. Americans easily deny their bloody colonial history and disguise wrongdoing as the work of a lone and abhorrent actor or as outsourced to malevolent corporations.

As the country awakened to the Civil Rights movement, people began to realize how the choice of what we eat is a political choice. Black Panthers in the 1970s set up a free lunch network in cities that fed children fresh fruit and vegetables instead of corporate processed foods. Religious and spiritual movements from India inspired vegetarian diets. On the whole, Americans came to discover that what advertisers were telling them wasn't in their best interest. A sugar advocacy council ad that proclaims the benefits of sugar consumption and rice council ads that use racist stereotypes were no longer accepted by a society that was opening itself to new ideas about what being an American means.

234

Corporations are still producing vast amounts of processed 'foods.' Advertising now invades every aspect of our life, occupying a grey area of entertainment and information. Nutritional research seems to contradict itself with each new study. What does all of this mean for the American stomach?

Advertising has historically adopted new technologies faster than consumers. Today, brands have identities and corporations are citizens. The brands themselves have become semantical shorthand that we use to signal to others our likes and social status. Food marketers no longer engage in the subtle business of encouraging the consumer to buy a product, but a long-term strategy to make loud overtures to their fans. Healthy and organic brands are most likely owned by the same corporation that owns the sugar-, fat- and salt-drenched junk food. Studies conducted by multiple universities have shown that the amount of synthesized flavors and salt, fats, and sugars in our processed foods have increased a thousand-fold. Our brains light up with pleasure when eating foods containing these things and the manufacturers know it.

Sugar Information, Inc. advertisement / 1970

Food magazines have abandoned print for online platforms where each features experts and celebrities preparing meals. Social media, especially Facebook and Instagram, feature QuickTime videos of people cooking recipes. Advertisers no longer purchase an ad but develop partnerships that directly sell their products through the content provider. The savvier we become as consumers, the more streamlined advertising has grown into our entertainment content. Advertising cookbooks are an antiquated method for teaching you how to eat.

Cookbooks aren't dead. The fastest growing segment of the publishing industry is cookbooks. Like those written in the 19th century, modern cookbooks are aspirational toward an idealized life of health and wealth. The books are written by successful chefs, famous stars, or the new phenomenon, the reality-cooking-show winner. The old appeal is there: we rely on experts to tell us how and what to eat while daydreaming of owning the kitchen, tools, and lifestyle of the wealthy 'stars.' Americans raised on generations of convenience consider cooking as a leisure activity. We buy cookbooks by the millions, but we're still eating frozen pizzas.

Food tells us who we are and who we want to be. Along our crooked path to becoming Americans, corporations, while reducing the amount of work it takes to make a meal, have also fed us a fair amount of garbage. Our emotional attachment to the foods we eat shouldn't stop us from making healthier choices. You should have access to and the ability to buy fresh foods. The people growing, harvesting, and making that food should be paid fairly. Pay attention to appeals to health or miraculous results of any food; they're not true. Don't believe claims that sound too good (or too bad) to be true; it's not true. It's okay to eat dessert once in a while. But please don't give babies soda pop. ★

Royal Salad Gelatin (Aspic)

The Headliner in Today's Food News!

Jellied Meats and Moulded Salads now as easy to make as a simple gelatin dessert

IT'S just what millions of women have been waiting for . . . this new, unsweetened Royal Salad Gelatin (Aspic), with its delicious meat-like flavor.

It simplifies the preparation of jellied meats and moulded salads . . . and these delicious foods, you know, are growing in popularity every day.

On a sultry, hot day, what is more tempting than a cool-looking mould of meat, fish or vegetables, sheathed in sparkling gelatin? It makes you *want* to eat—it's so invitingly chill.

For bridge luncheons and other special occasions, jellied good things bring more *ahs!* and *ahs!* than the most elaborate hot cooked food. They can be made the day before, too, or in the cool of the morning.

And they're so economical—for Royal Salad Gelatin makes a small amount of meat, fish or vegetables go a long way.

each for more than one person? With Royal Salad Gelatin, you can mould those bits of left-overs into a tempting dish that will serve six or eight people.

Look over these recipes. You'll almost surely find one that not only will use up what you have on hand, but will give you a dish as festive as any a master chef ever contrived.

Best of all—these tempting dishes are as easy to make as a simple gelatin dessert. Just dissolve a package of Royal Salad Gelatin in a cup of boiling water; add a cup of cold water. Chill until it thickens, mix in your other ingredients . . . chill until firm.

That's all. You don't have to use a fancy mould. A loaf pan can be used for any of these recipes.

If you want your dish to *look* fancy—that's easy, too. The pictures show how to do it . . . simply and quickly.

Uses up your Left-overs

What's in your refrigerator? A bit of left-over meat or fish? Cooked vegetables? A stalk or two of celery?

What if there *isn't* enough of

No meat stock to add

Remember, you don't have to add meat stock to Royal Salad Gelatin. It's ready for *instant* use, with a delicious meat-like flavor already in it.

Food Value of Royal Salad Gelatin (Aspic)—as Served

Per 100 grams of Salad Gelatin (as served)	Carbohy-drate	Protein	Fat	Calories
	4 grams	2 grams	No grams	24

31

Bibliography

A substantial percentage of writing is actually reading. In the food world, academic studies on nutrition, cultural movements, and actual history all play an essential part in telling this story. I'm indebted to all the people who have spent time in the dark corners of obscura working to uncover and document the thousands if not millions of left turns in food history.

The images are taken from my collection of advertising cookbooks. I'm grateful to the friends near and far who sent me favorite pieces from their personal collections. Feral House founder Adam Parfrey nagged this project into existence. He loved seeing images of crazy mid-century Jell-O® dishes and other abominations and wanted to publish something about them. We argued about what such a book should be. Adam saw the grossness and humor in the images while I knew that the real story was more sinister. He challenged me to write it my way. Adam spent hours on eBay buying up vintage advertising cookbooks he thought I could use for the project. I hadn't known the extent of his buying spree until I traveled to Port Townsend, Washington for his funeral. In the office, we found two boxes overflowing with booklets, pamphlets, and ephemera. Many of those are included in the image sections. For the record, Adam hated SPAM®.

- *100 Million Years of Food: What Our Ancestors Ate and Why It Matters Today*
  by Stephen Le (2016, Picador)

- *American Cookery: A Facsimile of the First Edition,*
  1796 by Amelia Simmons (1958, Oxford University Press)

- *American Food-What We've Cooked, How We've Cooked It, And The Ways We've Eaten In America Throughout The Centuries* by Evan Little (2007, The Overlook Press)

- *American Woman's Home Or Principles Of Domestic Science Being A Guide To The Formation And Maintenance Of Economical Healthful Beautiful And Christian Homes*
  by Catherine Beecher & Harriet Beecher Stowe (1869 unknown / Print on demand)

- *Aunt Jemima, Uncle Ben, and Rastus: Blacks in Advertising, Yesterday, Today, and Tomorrow*
  by Marilyn Kern Foxworth (1994, Praeger)

- *Bananas: An American History*
  by Virginia Scott Jenkins (2000, Smithsonian Books)

- *Bananas: How The United Fruit Company Shaped the World*
  by Peter Chapman (2007, Canongate)

- *The Banana Men: American Mercenaries and Entrepreneurs in Central America, 1880-1930*
  by Lester D. Langley (1995, University of Kentucky Press)

- *The Betrayal of Liliuokalani: Last Queen of Hawaii 1838-1917*
  by Helena G. Allen (1991, Mutual Publishing)

- *Bitter Fruit: The Story of the American Coup in Guatemala,*
  Revised and Expanded by Stephen Schlesinger
  (2005, David Rockefeller Center for Latin American Studies)

- *Canned: The Rise and Fall of Consumer Confidence in the American Food Industry*
  by Anna Zeide (2018, University of California Press)

- *Catherine Beecher: A Study in American Domesticity*
  by Katherine Kish Sklar (1976, W.W. Norton Company)

- *Dole Family History: Ancestors and Descendants of Wigglesworth Dole, Vol. 1*
  by Susan Dole Cole (2014, CreateSpace)

- *Empires of Food: Feast, Famine, and the Rise and Fall of Civilizations*
  by Evan D.G. Fraser (2012, Counterpoint)

- *The Fish That Ate the Whale: The Life and Times of America's Banana King*
  by Rich Cohen (2012, Picador)

- *Food on the Page: Cookbooks and American Culture*
  by Megan J. Elias (2017, University of Pennsylvania Press)

- *The Food Section: Newspaper Women and the Culinary Community*
  by Kim Wilmot Voss (2014, Rowman & Littlefield)

- *The Hidden Persuaders*
  by Vance Packard (1957 /2007 Ig Publishing)

- *A History of Cookbooks: From Kitchen to Page over Seven Centuries*
  by Henry Notaker (2017, University of California Press)

- *The History of the Puritans: Or, Protestant Nonconformists; from the Reformation in 1517, to the Revolution in 1688: Comprising an Account of Their Sufferings; and the Lives and Characters of Their Most Considerable Divines* by Daniel Neal (1822 unknown / 2018 (facsimile) Nabu Press)

- *Incredible Yanqui, The Career of Lee Christmas* by Hermann B. Deutsch (1931, Longsman, Green, & Co.)

- *Overthrow: America's Century of Regime Change From Hawaii to Iraq* by Stephen Kinzer (2006, Times Books/Henry Holt)

- *Paradox of Plenty: A Social History of Eating in Modern America* by Harvey Levenstein (1993 Oxford University Press/2003 University of California Press)

- *Perfection Salad: Women and Cooking at the Turn of the Century* by Laura Shapiro (1986 Farrar, Straus, and Giroux/2001 Modern Library)

- *Pineapple: A Global History* by Kaori O'Connor (2013, Reaktion Books)

- *Preserving on Paper: Seventeenth-Century Englishwomen's Receipt Books* by Kristine Kowalchuk (2017, University of Toronto Press)

- *Revolution at the Table: The Transformation of the American Diet* by Harvey Levenstein (1988 Oxford University Press/2003 University of California Press)

- *Sanford Ballard Dole: Hawaii's Only President, 1844-1926* by Helena G. Allen (1988, Arthur H. Clark)

- *Slave in a Box: The Strange Career of Aunt Jemima* by Maurice M. Manring (1998, University of Virginia Press)

- *SPAM®: A Biography: The Amazing True Story of America's "Miracle Meat"* by Carolyn Wyman (1999, Harvest Books)

- *Spuds, Spam® and Eating for Victory: Rationing in the Second World War* by Katherine Knight (2011, The History Press)

- *Stir It Up: Home Economics in American Culture* by Megan J. Elias (2010, University of Pennsylvania Press)

- *Swindled: The Dark History of Food Fraud, From Poisoned Candy to Counterfeit Coffee* by Bee Wilson (2008, Princeton University Press)

- *Three Squares: The Invention of the American Meal* by Abigail Carroll (2013, Basic Books)

- *Trust Us, We're Experts!* by Sheldon Rampton and John Stauber (2001, Tarcher/Putnam)

- *Understanding Jim Crow: Using Racist Memorabilia to Teach Tolerance and Promote Social Justice* by David Pilgrim (2015, PM Press)

- *Visible Saints: The History of a Puritan Idea* by Edmund Morgan (1963 unknown / 2013 (facsimile), Martino Fine Books)